Qur'an Made Easy

Surah 2

Al-Baqarah

By
Islamic Foundation

This book is dedicated to those seeking knowledge of Islam

Introduction to Surah Al-Baqarah

Surah Al-Baqarah is the longest Surah in the Qur'an; its virtues have been described in a multitude of hadiths and the benefits of reciting it are boundless. Prophet Muhammad [PBUH] stated:

> *"Everything has a hump (or, high peak), and Al-Baqarah is the high peak of the Qur'an. Whoever recites Al-Baqarah at night in his house, Shaytan will not enter that house for three nights. Whoever recites it during the day in his house, then Shaytan will not enter that house for three days."* [i]

Anyone who learns Surah Al-Baqarah and the 3rd Surah, Surah Al-Imran, will be protected on the Day of Resurrection; this is described in the following hadith where the Prophet Muhammad [PBUH] said:

> *"Learn Surah Al-Baqarah and Al-'Imran because they are two lights and they shade their people on the Day of Resurrection, just as two clouds, two spaces of shade or two lines of (flying) birds. The Qur'an will meet its companion in the shape of a pale-faced man on the Day of Resurrection when his grave is opened. The Qur'an will ask him: 'Do you know me?' The man will say: 'I do not know you.' The Qur'an will say: 'I am your companion, the Qur'an, which has brought you thirst during the heat and made you stay up during the night. Every merchant has his certain trade. But, this Day, you are behind all types of trade.'*

> *Kingship will then be given to him in his right hand, eternal life in his left hand and the crown of grace will be placed on his head. His parents will also be granted two garments that the people of this life could never afford. They will say: 'Why were we granted these garments?' It will be said: 'Because your son was carrying the Qur'an.' It will be said (to the reader of the Qur'an): 'Read and ascend through the levels of Paradise.' He will go on ascending as long as he recites, whether reciting slowly or quickly."* [ii]

There are many other virtues of reciting and learning and most importantly adhering to the commands and prohibitions stated in Surah Al-Baqarah, which we will go through in some detail.

The First Surah

2.1   Alif-Lam-Mim.

The first Verse in Surah Al-Baqarah are the letters Alif-Lam-Mim; only Allah knows the meanings of these letters and it is stated that they testify to the miracle of the Qur'an. In the Qur'an, no fewer than 29 Surahs begin with various letters, sometimes only two letters up to five letters.

Allah describes the believers

2.2   This is the Book (the Qur'an), whereof there is no doubt, a guidance to those who are Al-Muttaqun.

This Verse means that the Qur'an has been revealed from Allah and no one should doubt this. In later Verses the Qur'an challenges anyone to produce a Verse comparable to it, let alone the entire Qur'an, and this has and never will be achieved. Hence, the Qur'an is from Allah.

The second part of the above Verse states that the Qur'an is a guidance for the Muttaqun (which means the pious and righteous people who both fear Allah (and as a result refrain from all kinds of sins which He has forbidden) and love Allah (and as a result perform good deeds which He has ordained)). Hence, true guidance is only granted to those who have Taqwa (which means fear of Allah) and whilst a kafir who has great enmity to Islam can read the Qur'an, he will gain no benefit because his heart is devoid of accepting the message of Allah. However, those who seek guidance will be granted the knowledge of the Qur'an, by the Will of Allah, something that we see on a daily basis around the world with people from all other faiths accepting Islam in droves.

2.3   Who believe in the Ghaib and perform As-Salah, and spend out of what we have provided for them.

The word Ghaib means the unseen. Hence, a true believer is one who has faith in the unseen by the tongue, deed and creed[iii]. A true believer is one who believes in Allah, the angels, all the Prophet's that have been sent by Allah to carry His Message, who believe in the Hereafter, in the Day of Judgment, in both Paradise and Hell, in all the Books[iv] that were sent by the Messengers, without being able to see any of these (with the exception of the Qur'an, which is the only Book that has not been altered by man and is Allah's Divine Message that will never be changed, not even one word, until the end of time). The unseen covers all these points and many more.

The Salah as we have mentioned earlier is the prayer, although we need to elaborate on this further. The Arabic word Salah means 'supplication', meaning that by praying, we are supplicating to Allah. It should be performed according to the correct method, to complete the bowings, prostrations, recitation, humbleness before Allah, and punctual attendance for the prayer.[v]

The last part of the above, when it states 'and spend out of what we have provided for them' means the Zakah due on their wealth[vi].

2.4   And who believe in (the Qur'an and the Sunnah) which has been sent down to you (Muhammad [PBUH]) and in [the Taurat (Torah) and the Injeel (Gospel), etc.] which were sent down before you and they believe with certainty in the Hereafter.

The first part of this means that true Muslims believe in what Allah sent you with, and in what the previous Messengers were sent with, they do not distinguish between believing them, nor do they reject what they brought form their Lord[vii].

Although we believe that the books were sent to other messengers before Prophet Muhammad, these have been doctored by the people to such an extent that they cannot be relied upon. If we are faced with a situation when people quote other books to us, we are urged to follow the example of Prophet Muhammad [PBUH] who said:

> *"When the People of the Book narrate to you, neither reject nor affirm what they say. Rather, say: 'We believe in what was revealed to us and what was revealed to you.'"*[viii]

With regards to the second part of the above Verse where it mentions that they believe in the Hereafter with certainty, this refers to the resurrection, the standing on the Day of Resurrection, Paradise, the Fire, the reckoning and the Scale that weighs the deeds (which is called the Mizan)[ix].

2.5   They are on (true) guidance from their Lord, and they are the successful.

The people who are successful are those who follow all of the above; this means, they believe in the Unseen, perform the Salah on time and with all the conditions attached to the Salah, give Zakah to the poor, believe in the Books that Allah sent to the people through His Messengers, and believe in the Hereafter (meaning believe in the meeting with Allah, the reckoning, the scales, the Paradise and the Fire).

Allah describes the disbelievers

2.6   Verily, those who disbelieve, it is the same to them whether you (O Muhammad [PBUH]) warn them or do not warn them, they will not believe.

What the above Verse means is that for those whom Allah has decreed to be miserable in this life, nothing that Prophet Muhammad [PBUH] said to them would turn them towards the light. Hence, Prophet Muhammad [PBUH] was encouraged not to pity them.

2.7   Allah has set a seal on their hearts and on their hearings, and on their eyes there is a covering. Theirs will be a great torment.

Allah further describes the nature and characteristics of those who disbelieve. It has been stated that: "Shaytan controlled them when they obeyed him. Therefore, Allah sealed their hearts, hearing and sight, and they could neither see the guidance nor hear, comprehend or understand."[x]

Prophet Muhammad [PBUH] explained the different effects on the heart of a person as follows:

> *"When the believer commits a sin, a black dot will be engraved on his heart. If he repents, refrains and regrets, his heart will be polished again. If he commits more errors, the dots will increase until they cover his heart. This is the Ran (meaning stain) that Allah described."* [xi]

Allah describes the hypocrites

How hypocrisy began has been described in detail. When the Prophet Muhammad [PBUH] and the Muslims migrated from Makkah to Madinah to escape the persecutions and torture that the Quraysh were carrying out against them, they found two tribes (named Aws and Khazraj) who worshipped idols and three Jewish tribes who followed the books that their forefathers had doctored and altered.

Before the Muslims arrived, the tribes of Aws and Khazraj were about to appoint a man by the name of 'Abdullah bin Ubayy bin Salul as their leader, in effect their king. However, when the Muslims arrived, many of the tribes of Aws and Khazraj embraced Islam and as a result Ibn Salul's appointment as a king was thwarted.

Although outwardly he voiced his support for the Muslims, inwardly he developed a deep resentment and outright hatred for Islam. There were a few others who were promised worldly rewards before the advent of Islam who joined Ibn Salul.

This is how hypocrisy began.

During his time, Prophet Muhammad [PBUH] knew that Ibn Salul was a hypocrite and only pretended to be a Muslim. When one of the Companions asked Prophet Muhammad [PBUH] about the situation of Ibn Salul, he replied:

> *"I would not like the Arabs to say to each other that Muhammad is killing his Companions."[xii]*

However, such was the compassion of Prophet Muhammad [PBUH] and his desire to bring everyone in the fold of Islam and to seek their forgiveness, that when Ibn Salul died, Prophet Muhammad [PBUH] performed the funeral prayer for him. When he was asked why he prayed for him, he replied:

"If I knew that by asking (Allah to forgive Ibn Salul) more than seventy times that He would forgive him, I would do that." [xiii]

Allah begins describing the hypocrites in the following Verses of the Qur'an:

2.8   And of mankind, there are some (hypocrites) who say: "We believe in Allah and the Last Day" while in fact they believe not.

2.9   They try to deceive Allah and those who believe, while they only deceive themselves, and perceive (it) not!

The above Verses describe the characteristics of a hypocrite. This has been further elaborated as follows: "This is the description of a hypocrite. He is devious, he says the truth with his tongue and defies it with his heart and deeds. He wakes up in a condition other than the one he goes to sleep in, and goes to sleep in a different condition than the one he wakes up in. He changes his mind just like a ship that moves about whenever a wind blows."[xiv]

> **2.10   In their hearts is a disease (of doubt and hypocrisy) and Allah has increased their disease. A painful torment is theirs because they used to tell lies.**

The hypocrites have two characteristics: they tell lies and they deny the Unseen.

> **2.11   And when it is said to them: "Make not mischief on the earth," they say: "We are only peacemakers."**

> **2.12   Verily! They are the ones who make mischief, but they perceive not.**

When the above Verse states, 'Do not make mischief on the earth,' what it means is: "Do not commit acts of disobedience on the earth. Their mischief is disobeying Allah, because whoever disobeys Allah on the earth, or commands that Allah be disobeyed, he has committed mischief on the earth. Peace on both the earth and in the heavens is ensured (and earned) through obedience to Allah."[xv]

It has also been stated that, "They give as much aid as they can, against Allah's loyal friends, and support those who deny Allah, His Books and His Messengers. This is how the hypocrites commit mischief on earth."[xvi]

> **2.13   And when it is said to them: "Believe as the people (followers of Muhammad [PBUH]) have believed," they say: "Shall we believe as the fools have believed?" Verily, they are the fools, but they know not.**

When the hypocrites said, 'Shall we believe as the fools have believed?' they are referring to the Companions of Prophet Muhammad [PBUH]. However, Allah confirms that the hypocrites are indeed the fools but they perceive not since they are so ignorant and so far from the path of righteousness.

> **2.14   And when they meet those who believe, they say: "We believe," but when they are alone with their Shayatin (devils – meaning polytheists, hypocrites, leaders amongst the rabbis of the Jews etc.), they say: "Truly, we are with you; verily, we were but mocking."**

> **2.15   Allah mocks at them and gives them increase in their wrong-doings to wander blindly.**

The above Verses testify that amongst the devils, there are both human devils and Jinn devils. This is confirmed in Surah 6, Verse 112 which states: "And so We have appointed for every Prophet enemies - Shayatin (devils) among mankind and jinns, inspiring one another with adorned speech as a delusion (or by way of deception)."

Hence, both Jinn devils and human devils are present amongst us and they work to turn the Muslims from the path of Allah.

What is meant by mocking in the above Verse? It means "we only mock the believers and deceive them."[xvii]

However, Allah counters them by stating that He mocks them. How Allah does that is described in Surah 3, Verse 178, which states: "And let not the disbelievers think that Our postponing of their punishment is good for them. We postpone the punishment only so that they may increase in sinfulness. And for them is a disgracing torment." Prophet Muhammad [PBUH] added:

"This, and its like, is Allah's mockery of the hypocrites and the people of Shirk."[xviii]

There are many other Verses in the Qur'an which confirms that by giving the hypocrites and the disbelievers worldly possessions in this life, they are not exempt from obeying the commands of Allah; by thinking they have these possessions, the hypocrites and disbelievers continue in their transgression but ultimately they will be held accountable on the Day of Resurrection.

2.16 These are they who have purchased error for guidance, so their commerce was profitless. And they were not guided.

The hypocrites gave up the truth and deviated into misguidance and hence, their trade was not successful. What is meant by 'And they were not guided' has been described by Qatadah as: "I have seen them leaving guidance for deviation, leaving the Jama'ah (the community of the believers) for the sects, leaving safety for fear, and the Sunnah for innovation."[xix]

2.17 Their likeness is as the likeness of one who kindled a fire; then, when it illuminated all around him, Allah took away their light and left them in darkness. (So) they could not see.

2.18 They are deaf, dumb, and blind, so they return not (to the right path).

In the above Verse, Allah gives the first of two parables of the hypocrites; they are referred to as the 'complete hypocrites' whose light is taken away and they are left in complete darkness.

What is meant by light above is what benefits a person, and what is meant by darkness are the doubts, disbelief and hypocrisy. Hence, the above Verse can be read as: 'Allah took away what benefits them and left them in their disbelief and doubts. And they are unable to find the correct path.'

And the hypocrites are deaf (meaning they cannot hear the guidance), dumb (meaning they cannot utter the words that might benefit them) and blind (meaning they are in total darkness and deviation).

2.19   Or like a rainstorm from the sky, wherein is darkness, thunder, and lightning. They thrust their fingers in their ears to keep out the stunning thunderclap for fear of death. But Allah ever encompasses the disbelievers (i.e. Allah will gather them all together).

2.20   The lightning almost snatches away their sight, whenever it flashes for them, they walk therein, and when darkness covers them, they stand still. And if Allah willed, He could have taken away their hearing and their sight. Certainly, Allah has power over all things.

This is the second parable that Allah provides of the hypocrites, and these are referred to as the 'hesitant hypocrites'.

The hypocrites are usually full of fear and anxiety (which relates to the thunder in the above Verse); the lightning refers to the light of faith that is sometimes evident in the hearts of the hypocrites. But whatever they do (i.e. thrusting their fingers in their ears), they cannot escape the fear that they usually feel.

The second Verse means: "Whenever the hypocrites acquire a share in the victories of Islam, they are content with this share. Whenever Islam suffers a calamity, they are ready to revert to disbelief."[xx]

It also refers to the Day of Judgment; on that Day, every person must cross the Sirat (which is the bridge over the Fire). Each person will be given a light, which will shine, for the person according to their degree of faith. The strong believers will be given a light that will stretch several miles, others less. Some people will have a light that will go out and come back and continue to do so, whilst they are trying to cross the Sirat. Some people will have no light at all and they are the hypocrites.

Hence, from the above four verses, the parable of the fire are the complete hypocrites (those who will be left in complete darkness) whereas the parable of the rainstorm are the hesitant hypocrites (those who have a small degree of faith on occasions).

In addition, the hypocrites have been referred to as 'pure hypocrites' and 'those that have some hypocrisy in them' as is described by the Prophet Muhammad [PBUH]:

> *"Whoever has the following three (characteristics) will be a pure hypocrite, and whoever has one of the following three characteristics will have one characteristic of hypocrisy, unless and until he gives it up. Whenever he speaks, he tells a lie. Whenever he makes a covenant, he proves treacherous. Whenever he is entrusted, he breaches the trust."* [xxi]

Tawhid Al-Uluhiyyah

2.21   **O mankind! Worship your Lord (Allah), Who created you and those who were before you so that you may acquire Taqwa.**

2.22   **Who has made the earth a resting place for you, and the sky as a canopy, and sent down water (rain) from the sky and brought forth therewith fruits as a provision for you. Then do not set up rivals unto Allah (in worship) while you know (that He Alone has the right to be worshipped).**

In the above Verses Allah describes His Oneness in divinity, that only He who created every soul, should be worshipped. In addition, Allah states the countless favors that He has blessed the people with, some of which are apparent and some hidden. He is the Creator of everything, the Sustainer of everything, the Owner of everything, and the Provider of everything in this life. Hence, the people should not worship anyone or anything else besides Allah. The prohibition of setting up rivals with Allah is one of the cornerstones of Islam and has been mentioned in several Verses of the Qur'an.

The Quran is the Truth

2.23   And if you (Arab pagans, Jews, and Christians) are in doubt concerning that which We have sent down (i.e. the Qur'an) to Our servant (Muhammad [PBUH]), then produce a Surah (chapter) of the like thereof and call your witnesses (supporters and helpers) besides Allah, if you are truthful.

2.24   But if you do it not, and you can never do it, then fear the Fire (Hell) whose fuel is men and stones, prepared for the disbelievers.

Allah states that the Qur'an is the truth! However, if anyone disagrees with this, Allah has challenged them to produce a similar Surah if they are truthful. And Allah has challenged the people whether as individuals or in groups; however, no one has been able to do this for over 1,400 years and no one will be able to do this because the Qur'an is the word of Allah. And Allah has guaranteed that the Qur'an will not be altered or changed and it will be preserved by Allah until the end of time.

The Qur'an is also described as the greatest miracle given to Prophet Muhammad [PBUH] for he said:

> *"Every Prophet was given a miracle, the type of which brings mankind to faith. What I was given is a revelation that Allah sent down to me. Yet, I hope that I will have the most following on the Day of Resurrection."[xxii]*

Allah warns that anyone who doubts the Qur'an should fear Hell whose fuel is men and stones. The stones mentioned in the Verse have been described as giant, rotten, black, sulphuric stones – they become the hottest when heated; every disbeliever who ends up in hell will be burnt and experience pain the likes of which no one will experience during their lives. May Allah save us from this and may Allah keep us away from Hell.

The Arabic name of Hellfire is Jahannam and many scholars are of the opinion that it exists now. For example, the Prophet Muhammad [PBUH] stated in a hadith:

> *"Paradise and the Fire had an argument . . ."[xxiii]*

We already know that Paradise exists because Prophet Adam, Eve and Iblis were expelled from it onto the earth, hence according to the above hadith, Hellfire also exists now. The following hadith corroborates this as Prophet Muhammad [PBUH] explained the sound that the Companions heard which was of a falling object:

> *"This is a stone that was thrown from the top of Jahannam seventy years ago, but only now reached its bottom."[xxiv]*

The righteous believers will be rewarded

2.25   **And give glad tidings to those who believe and do righteous good deeds, that for them will be Gardens under which rivers flow (Paradise). Every time they will be provided with a fruit therefrom, they will say: "This is what we were provided with before," and they will be given things in resemblance (i.e. in the same form but different in taste) and they shall have therein Azwajun Mutahharatun (purified mates or wives), and they will abide therein forever.**

In the previous Verses, Allah described the torment that the disbelievers will face in the Hereafter; in this Verse Allah describes the good things that the believers will be rewarded with. This is why the Qur'an was called Mathani, meaning where it mentions belief and then disbelief or vice versa.

Allah states that the believers will be rewarded with Paradise where the rivers run beneath its trees and rooms, not in valleys. Prophet Muhammad [PBUH] has a lake in Paradise, which is called Al-Kawthar which is made of dome of hollow pearls.

What else do we know of Paradise? "The grass of Paradise is made of saffron, its hills from musk and the boys of everlasting youth will serve the believers with fruits which they will eat. They will then be brought similar fruits, and the people of Paradise will comment: 'This is the same as what you have just brought us.' The boys will say to them: 'Eat, for the color is the same, but the taste is different.'"[xxv]

In Paradise, the people will be given fruits to eat: "They are similar to the fruits of this life, but the fruits of Paradise taste better."[xxvi]

The believers will also be granted Azwajun Mutahharatun which means mates and wives who are purified from filth and impurity and sin, and free from menstruation, relieving the call of nature, urine, spit, semen and pregnancies.[xxvii]

The final part of the above Verse confirms that the believers will enjoy the fruits and goodness of Paradise forever because their existence in Paradise will never cease or end.

Allah refutes the hypocrites' claim of misleading parables

2.26 **Verily, Allah is not ashamed to set forth a parable even of a mosquito or so much more when it is bigger (or less when it is smaller) than it. And as for those who believe, they know that it is the Truth from their Lord, but as for those who disbelieve, they say: "What did Allah intend by this parable?" By it He misleads many, and many He guides thereby. And He misleads thereby only those who are Al-Fasiqun (the rebellious, disobedient to Allah).**

2.27 **Those who break Allah's Covenant after ratifying it, and sever what Allah has ordered to be joined and do mischief on earth, it is they who are the losers.**

The above Verses were revealed by Allah as a result of the following:

When Allah revealed the two parables of the hypocrites, that of the kindling a fire (Verses 2.17 and 2.18) and the rainstorm from the sky (Verses 2.19 and 2.20), the hypocrites proclaimed that Allah was too great and too exalted to have made such examples[xxviii]. However, Allah refuted the hypocrites with the above Verses by stating that He can and will provide any examples as He chooses, even using the parable of a mosquito, which is one of the most insignificant and tiniest of creatures.

And as is stated above, the hypocrites will use any excuse not to believe in Allah and His Message, the Qur'an. Allah has described these people in the Qur'an as Al-Fasiqun, meaning they are rebellious and disobedient to Allah.

As for the believers, it is stated that: "The believers believe in these parables, whether they involve large matters or small, because they know that they are the truth from their Lord, and Allah guides the believers by these parables."[xxix]

With regards to those who break Allah's covenant, this means the disbelievers and the hypocrites of the people of the Book and how they were informed in their Books about the coming of Prophet Muhammad [PBUH] and they swore to Allah to believe in him when he was sent. However, when Allah sent Prophet Muhammad [PBUH], they rejected him and his message and threw the Books that stated the coming of Prophet Muhammad [PBUH] and altered the words in their hand-written versions that omitted the coming of Prophet Muhammad [PBUH]. May Allah curse the disbelievers and hypocrites of the people of the Book for their rejection of Prophet Muhammad [PBUH] and the Divine Message that Allah sent.

2.28 **How can you disbelieve in Allah? Seeing that you were dead and He gave you life. Then He will give you death, then again will bring you to life (on the Day of Resurrection) and then unto Him you will return.**

The beginning of creation

2.29   He it is Who created for you all that is on earth. Then He Istawa (rose over) towards the heaven and made them seven heavens and He is the All-Knower of everything.

Allah begins describing the beginning of Creation. This is further explained in Surah 41, Verses 9 to 12; a summary of it and a breakdown of the different days of creation are described below[xxx]:

Allah created the Earth in 2 days, meaning Sunday and Monday. This is how buildings are usually formed, with the foundation being built first and the upper floors next.
Then, Allah created the heaven.
Then, Allah spread the earth out and provided the provisions for growth, this being on Tuesday and Wednesday. Daha – the treasures of the Earth were brought to the surface; the water burst onto its surface and the plants grew; the stars began rotating, as did the planets.
Allah then completed creating the 7 heavens in 2 more days, these being Thursday and Friday.

We will discuss the creation of everything as we go through the Qur'an.

The story of Prophet Adam, the angels and Iblis

2.30   And (remember) when your Lord said to the angels: "Verily, I am going to place (mankind) generations after generations on earth." They said: "Will You place therein those who will make mischief therein and shed blood, - while we glorify You with praises and thanks and sanctify You." He (Allah) said: "I know that which you do not know."

In the next ten Verses (2.30 to 2.39) the Qur'an describes the story of Prophet Adam, and angels and Iblis.

When Allah informed the angels that He was going to create man and place mankind generations after generations on the earth, the angels asked: "Will you place therein those who will make mischief therein and shed blood." The angels were not being haughty when they asked Allah the question; they knew from the behavior of other creatures who had lived on the Earth before humans were created, particularly the behavior of the jinn, that not all creatures would worship Allah as they had done.

And when the angels said: "while we glorify You with praises and thanks and sanctify You." By this the angels were requesting that they be given the honor of inhabiting the earth instead of man.

However, Allah refutes the request from the angels by stating: "I know that which you do not know." Allah replied to the angels that He knew the benefit of creating a creature such as a human and they did not, and that the benefit would outweigh the harm that they referred to. He explained that He would send the people of the Earth prophets and messengers, righteous people and martyrs; these noble people among Allah's servants would teach the people, guiding them between right and wrong.

Some scholars[xxxi] have also used Verse 2.30 as evidence that it is an obligation to appoint a Khalifah to pass judgments on matters of dispute between people, judge between the oppressor and the oppressed, and ultimately to apply the Islamic code.

But who should be the Khalifah and how is he appointed?

There are certain characteristics that a Khalifah must have: he must be an adult Muslim male, bodily able, righteous, has knowledge of warfare of politics, and has the knowledge to perform Ijtihad (which means independent legal judgments). It is also stated that he must be from the tribe of Quraysh although not necessarily from the tribe of Bani Hashim.

As for the appointment of a Khalifah, this can be done in a number of ways: he can either be named by a group of scholars (this is how Abu Bakr was appointed Khalifah after Prophet Muhammad [PBUH]) or the current Khalifah appoints a successor (as Abu Bakr did with 'Umar), or the Khalifah leaves the decision to the Muslim consultative council or a group of righteous men (as 'Umar did with 'Uthman).

> **2.31** **And He taught Adam all the names (of everything), then He showed them to the angels and said: "Tell Me the names of these if you are truthful."**

> **2.32** **They (angels) said: "Glory be to You, we have no knowledge except what you have taught us. Verily, it is You, the All-Knower, the All-Wise."**

> **2.33** **He said: "O Adam! Inform them of their names," and when he had informed them of their names, He said: "Did I not tell you that I know the Ghaib (unseen) in the heavens and the earth, and I know what you reveal and what you have been concealing?"**

Allah taught Adam the names of everything, including "the names that people use such as human, animal, sky, earth, land, sea, horse, donkey and so forth, including the names of the other species."[xxxii] It has also been stated that Allah taught him the names of the plate and the pot and even the terms for breaking wind.[xxxiii]

And when the angels could not name them, Allah commanded Adam to tell the angels the names of everything. Allah then informed the angels that only He had knowledge of the unseen in the heavens and the earth, and only He had knowledge of what the angels were revealing and what they were hiding.

2.34 **And (remember) when We said to the angels: "Prostrate yourselves before Adam." And they prostrated except Iblis (Satan), he refused and was proud and was one of the disbelievers (disobedient to Allah).**

When Allah commanded the angels to prostrate before Adam, Iblis was included in this even though he was not an angel. There are certain misconceptions that Iblis was an angel, or a fallen angel; however, Iblis was a jinn[xxxiv] and even more than that, he was one of their leaders. Before he attained the notorious name of Iblis or Satan, he was commonly referred to as 'Azazeel.

It is worth extrapolating on the Jinn and Iblis a little further.

The jinn inhabited the Earth 2,000 years prior to man and when they committed corruption on the Earth and shed blood, they were banished to small lands by a group of angels whom Allah had sent. There is a difference of opinion as to the part played by Iblis in this chain of events. One theory holds that Iblis was amongst the other jinn on the Earth and when the angels were sent by Allah to drive the jinn to the islands, he was captured by the angels and taken to the heavens. Another theory holds that it was Iblis, at the head of the angels, who was sent to drive the other jinn to the remote islands. Allah knows best.

What is without a doubt is that Iblis was extremely knowledgeable which was a blessing that Allah had bestowed upon him; however, his sharp mind made him arrogant and haughty to those he considered inferior to him. This provides evidence that the first error, hence the first sin ever committed was arrogance. Iblis' knowledge had made him arrogant and for this reason he disobeyed Allah.

Regarding arrogance, this is an evil sin and Prophet Muhammad [PBUH] commented on this as follows:

> *"No person who has the weight of a mustard seed of arrogance in his heart shall enter Paradise."[xxxv]*

Hence, due to his arrogance, Iblis disobeyed Allah and refused to bow before Adam.

Regarding prostrating before a person, this was permitted for previous nations but was abrogated when Prophet Muhammad [PBUH] was sent with the final message, the Qur'an. It has been stated in a hadith that Mu'adh said to the Prophet Muhammad [PBUH]:

> *"I visited Ash-Sham and found that they used to prostrate before their priests and scholars. You, O Messenger of Allah, are more deserving of prostration."*

> *The Prophet [PBUH] said: "No. If I was to command any human to prostrate before another human, I would command the wife to prostrate before her husband because of the enormity of his right on her."[xxxvi]*

We will discuss how Allah expelled Iblis from His presence in Surah 7, Verses 13 to 18.

2.35   **And We said: "O Adam! Dwell you and your wife in the Paradise and eat both of you freely with pleasure and delight of things therein as wherever you will, but come not near this tree or you both will be of the Zalimun (wrong-doers)."**

2.36   **Then the Shaytan made them slip therefrom (the Paradise), and got them out from that in which they were. We said: "Get you down, all, with enmity between yourselves. On earth will be a dwelling place for you and an enjoyment for a time."**

Allah permitted Adam and Hawwa to live in Paradise. There is a difference of opinion as to where this Paradise was, with one view saying that this was on the Earth. However, the majority of the view of scholars, and in the view of renowned Islamic scholar Ibn Kathir and his book Al-Bidayah wan-Nihayah, the Paradise where Adam and Hawwa lived, was in heaven called Jannatul-Ma'wa (the Garden of Eternal Abode).

Whilst living in Paradise, they were both given strict instructions that they could eat as they pleased; one particular tree, however, was off-bounds to them. They were commanded not to eat from it. It has been said that it was the Tree of Eternity, known as Shajarat Al-Khuld. Prophet Muhammad [PBUH] said:

> *"Verily, in Paradise there is a tree which a rider can travel under its shade for one hundred years and still not have passed it. It is the Tree of Eternity."[xxxvii]*

However, Shaytan lured them towards the tree with false promises that if they ate from the tree they would be rewarded with eternal life and that they would become angels; he also promised them that their dominion would not waste away. The majority of scholars have stated that Shaytan was prohibited from entering Paradise, but to enter it and to cause mischief during the period of his respite which will continue until the Day of Judgment, he would at times sneak into Paradise in secret. It is also said that he hid inside the mouth of the snake when it entered Paradise, and this is probably the reason why there are many hadiths on the benefits of killing snakes[xxxviii].

When Adam and Hawwa ate from the tree (it was said that it was Hawwa who ate from the tree first), their garments were stripped from them and their private parts became naked. In their embarrassment, they quickly covered themselves with fig leaves.

Prophet Muhammad [PBUH] added:

> *"Adam was a tall man, about the height of a palm tree, and he had thick hair on his head. When he committed the error that he committed, his private part appeared to him while before he did not see it. So he started running in fright through Paradise, but a tree in Paradise took him by the head. He said to it, 'Release me,' but it said, 'No, I will not release you.' So his Lord called him, 'O Adam! Do you run away from Me?' He said, 'O Lord! I felt ashamed before you.'"[xxxix]*

Adam then repented to Allah as is stated in the next Verse:

2.37   **Then Adam received from his Lord Words. And his Lord pardoned him (accepted his repentance). Verily, He is the One Who forgives (accepts repentance), the Most Merciful.**

This means that a person will be forgiven for repenting, but only if it is sincere repentance. This is vital because Shaytan was given respite to tempt humans towards evil and disobey Allah, which he will continue to do until the Day of Judgment.

2.38   **We said: "Get down all of you from this place (the Paradise), then whenever there comes to you Hudan (guidance) from Me, and whoever follows My Guidance, there shall be no fear on them, nor shall they grieve.**

2.39   **But those who disbelieve and belie Our Ayat (proofs, evidences, verses, lessons, signs, revelations, etc.) such are the dwellers of the Fire, they shall abide therein forever."**

Those who follow the guidance, and therefore the Qur'an and the Sunnah of Prophet Muhammad [PBUH], they will be successful both in this life and the Hereafter; however, those who defy the command of Allah and do not follow the Qur'an and the Final Messenger, they will end up in the Fire and they will remain there forever.

The children of Israel

2.40   **O Children of Israel! Remember My Favor which I bestowed upon you, and fulfill (your obligations to) My Covenant (with you) so that I fulfill (My Obligations to) your covenant (with Me), and fear none but Me.**

2.41   **And believe in what I have sent down (this Qur'an), confirming that which is with you, (the Tawrah and the Injeel), and be not the first to disbelieve therein, and buy not with My Verses [the Tawrah and the Injeel) a small price (i.e. getting a small gain by selling My Verses), and fear Me and Me Alone.**

What are the favors that Allah blessed upon the Children of Israel? Firstly, Allah blessed them by sending Prophets and Messengers amongst them and revealing Books to them. Also, Allah saved the Children of Israel again and again and again, from persecution and hunger and starvation – these have been detailed in the Stories of the Prophets by Ibn Kathir.

What was Allah's Covenant with the Children of Israel? The Covenant has been described as follows: "My covenant that I took from you concerning Prophet Muhammad [PBUH], when he sent to you, so that I grant you what I promised you if you believe in him and follow him. I will then remove the chains and restrictions that were placed around your necks, because of the errors that you committed."[xl]

On a related point, why were the Children of Israel called the 'Children of Israel'? This is because Israel is Prophet Ya'qub (known in the Bible and Tawrah as Prophet Jacob). It has been stated in a hadith:

> "A group of Jews came to the Prophet [PBUH] and he said to them: "Do you know that Israel is Ya'qub?" They said: "Yes, by Allah." He said: "O Allah! Be witness."[xli]

It has also been stated that Israel means 'the servant of Allah'.[xlii]

Allah also commanded the Children of Israel to follow the Qur'an and to follow the Message of Prophet Muhammad [PBUH], which was divinely revealed by Allah the Almighty, and not to sell the Verses of the Qur'an cheaply.

2.42   **And mix not truth with falsehood, nor conceal the truth while you know (the truth).**

2.43   **And perform As-Salat, and give Zakat, and bow down along with Ar-Raki'in.**

Allah commanded the Jews not to mix Judaism and Christianity with Islam, and not to hide the knowledge that they had in their Books of Prophet Muhammad [PBUH] and what he was sent with.

Allah also commanded the people of the Book to perform the Salah (the prayer) and to give Zakah (giving charity to the poor) and to bow down with the Al-Raki'in (meaning to bow down with those who bow down among the Ummah of Prophet Muhammad [PBUH]).

Practice what you preach

2.44   Enjoin you Al-Birr (piety and righteousness and every act of obedience to Allah) on the people and you forget (to practice it) yourselves, while you recite the Scripture (the Tawrah)! Have you then no sense?

This has been best explained as follows: "This is about the People of the Book and the hypocrites. They used to command people to pray and fast. However, they did not practice what they commanded others. Allah reminded them of this behavior. So whoever commands people to do righteousness, let him be among the first of them to implement that command."[xliii]

Prophet Muhammad [PBUH] commented on those who do not practice what they preach, which is described in the following hadith:

"A man will be brought on the Day of Resurrection and thrown in the Fire. His intestines will fall out and he will continue circling pulling them behind him, just as the donkey goes around the pole. The people of the Fire will go to that man and ask him: 'What happened to you? Did you not used to command us to do righteous acts and forbid us from committing evil?' He will say: 'Yes. I used to enjoin righteousness, but refrained from performing righteousness, and I used to forbid you to perform from evil while I myself did it.'"[xliv]

Patience and prayer

2.45   **And seek help in patience and As-Salat (the prayer) and truly it is extremely heavy and hard except for Al-Khashi'in.**

2.46   **(They are those) who are certain that they are going to meet their Lord, and that unto Him they are going to return.**

Allah commands his believing servants to seek His help with patience and the prayer.

What is meant by patience in the above Verse is to fast; this is also the reason why Ramadan is called the month of patience[xlv].

The Salah is one of the best and most important methods of adhering to Allah's commands.

Allah describes the Al-Khashi'in as those who believe in what He has revealed[xlvi], and these are the loyal servants of Allah who stick to His commands, especially the Salat and fasting. And these are the people who are certain that they are going to meet Allah on the Day of Resurrection and are certain in the Hereafter. This has been illustrated by the following hadith: "on the Day of Resurrection Allah will say to a servant: "Have I not allowed you to marry, honored you, made the horses and camels subservient to you and allowed you to become a chief and a master" He will say: "Yes." Allah will say: "Did you have Zann (meaning think) that you will meet Me?" He will say: "No." Allah will say: "This Day, I will forget you, just as you forgot Me.""[xlvii]

The children of Israel were favored by Allah

2.47 **O Children of Israel! Remember My Favor which I bestowed upon you and that I preferred you to the 'Alamin (mankind and jinns) (of your time).**

The above Verse again highlights that Allah favored the Children of Israel over others during their time, by sending them Prophets and Messengers from among them, by sending them Books, and by saving them from destruction and destitution time and time again.

Although the Children of Israel were favored during their time, the Ummah of Prophet Muhammad [PBUH] is better than the Children of Israel, which has been described in Surah 3, Verse 110, and also by the following hadith in which the Prophet Muhammad [PBUH] said:

"You (Muslims) are the seventieth nation, but you are the best and most honored of them according to Allah."[xlviii]

Fear the Day of Judgment

2.48　　**And fear a Day (of Judgment) when a person shall not avail another, nor will intercession be accepted from him nor will compensation be taken from him nor will they be helped.**

This Verse highlights that on the Day of Judgment, each person will stand alone; they cannot seek help or assistance from anyone else and nobody can intercede on their behalf. And not a single person will be able to ransom themselves, meaning buy or bribe their way out of being judged by the wealth they have accumulated in this life.

The story of Prophet Musa (AS)

2.49   **And (remember) when We delivered you from Fir'awn's (Pharaoh) people, who were afflicting you with a horrible torment, killing your sons and sparing your women, and therein was a mighty trial from your Lord.**

The story of Prophet Musa has been well documented in several Verses of the Qur'an. Below we provide the most accurate version according to Ibn Kathir's Stories of the Prophets and the tafsir of the Qur'an.

Egypt was the land of the Fir'awns who commanded incredible power over their subjects and ruled with absolute authority. At the time of Musa's birth, the Fir'awn was one of the evilest tyrants to ever rule the Earth. He ruled over not just the Egyptian Copts but also the Children of Israel, who had been living in Egypt for 400 years. The Fir'awn ordered the Children of Israel, who were the best people of their time, to live a life of misery; they were tasked with the worst jobs, including hard labor, and were humiliated daily.

One day the evil Fir'awn had a dream in which he saw a fire coming from Bait Al-Maqdis, the masjid in Jerusalem; the fire entered the houses of all the Egyptian Copts and burned them. However, the fire did not touch the houses of the Israelites. The Fir'awn was greatly distressed by his dream and immediately called his priests, his soothsayers and his sorcerers. He asked them to interpret his dream. After discussing it amongst themselves they said it was a prophecy in which a boy borne to the Children of Israel would rise up and destroy his kingdom.

The Fir'awn was so distraught by the response of his advisors that he ordered one of the cruelest punishments in the history of the world. He ordered that all male children born to the Israelites should be murdered, whilst the girls would be permitted to live.

How Fir'awn carried out his wicked plan needs to be explained further.

The Fir'awn appointed midwives to keep a check on the Israelite women; when one of them became pregnant, the midwives would write their names down on their ledger. The midwives used coercion and blackmail to get people to spy on their neighbors; this caused distrust and enmity amongst the people. When the time approached for the pregnant woman to give birth, the midwives would visit her regularly and monitor her. When she went into labor, only the midwife was allowed to be with her and all family and friends were forced to leave; even the woman's husband and her mother were not allowed to be in the same room as her. In this helpless state, the woman would give birth. If she gave birth to a girl, the baby would be left with her and her family were then permitted to see her. However, if she gave birth to a boy, the midwife would tell the guards waiting outside; they would enter the room with their knives and swords drawn and would murder the baby boy in cold blood. By this action alone, the Fir'awn earned a place in history as one of the evilest men to have ever lived.

This carried on year after year, and with each passing year the number of young girls began to increase and young boys began to decrease. The Egyptian Copts realized that if this continued, when the children of the Israelites got older, there would not be enough of them to carry out the menial and humiliating jobs that they were currently doing and ultimately this burden would fall upon the Egyptian Copts. As a result, they spoke with the Fir'awn and he agreed to lessen the burden; he ordered that boys borne to Israelite woman would be murdered not every year, but every other year.

In these turbulent times a baby boy was born to an Israelite woman. The boy was in fact the one that the Fir'awn had feared; his name was Musa. When his mother fell pregnant, by the Will of Allah she did not show the signs of pregnancy. When she gave birth to Musa and she realized it was a boy, she became extremely fearful for his survival. However, no one outside her family realized this and anyone who did come into contact with him, they immediately fell in love with him.

2.50 And (remember) when We separated the sea for you and saved you and drowned Fir'awn's (Pharaoh) people while you were watching.

Allah commanded Musa to strike the sea with his staff. When he had done so, the sea cleft asunder and was split into twelve paths, one path for each of the twelve tribes of the Israelites. Allah then commanded the wind, which blew across each path, drying it thereby making it easier to walk across.

The Israelites followed Musa and began crossing the sea to the other side, each tribe following its designated path, to the safety of the other side. By the time the last of the Israelites had reached the other side, Fir'awn and his army arrived at the edge of the shore.

When Fir'awn saw the sea and how it had parted to reveal twelve dry paths, he was both astonished and frightened. The wall of sea on each side was like a mountain and Fir'awn did not want to follow the Israelites across the path for fear that the sea would collapse on top of him.

However, Allah sent the angel Jibril who came towards Fir'awn on a war stallion and passed by Fir'awn's horse. When Jibril's horse whinnied at Fir'awn's horse, the latter rushed into one of the dry paths between the sea; in sheer desperation, Fir'awn tried to pull the reigns of his horse to hold him back. But it was too late! His horse galloped into the sea.

Allah sent the angel Mika'il to the rear of Fir'awn's huge army; he began pushing the entire army into the sea. Fir'awn and his army were now galloping through the dry paths in haste.

By the time Fir'awn was about to reach the other side, to where Musa and the Israelites stood watching, his entire army was on the dry paths with the sea on either side of them.

At this point, Allah caused the sea to collapse over them.

Having been under the tyranny of the Fir'awns for 400 hundred years, the Israelites could not believe that Fir'awn had been destroyed; the Fir'awn had committed horrendous crimes against them and their baby sons who were murdered in cold blood with swords and carving knives. And when he drowned, they initially doubted that he had finally gone. Allah assured them of his death as is described in Surah 10, Verse 92 and also in the following hadith:

> *"Some of the Children of Israel doubted the death of Fir'awn so Allah commanded the sea to throw his body – whole, without a soul, with his known armor plate. The body was thrown to a high place on the land so that the Children of Israel could confirm his death and destruction."[xlix]*

The day that the Children of Israel were rescued from Fir'awn has been named the Day of 'Ashura. It has narrated in a hadith that:

> *"The Prophet came to Madinah and saw the Jews fasting on the day of Ashura. He asked them about that. They replied: "This is a good day, the day on which Allah rescued the Children of Israel from their enemy. So, Musa fasted this day." The Prophet said: "We have more claim over Musa than you." So, the Prophet fasted on that day and ordered (the Muslims) to fast (on that day)."[l]*

The children of Israel worship the calf

2.51   And (remember) when We appointed for Musa forty nights, and (in his absence) you took the calf (for worship), and you were Zalimun (polytheists and wrong-doers).

2.52   Then after that We forgave you so that you might be grateful.

2.53   And (remember) when We gave Musa the Scripture (the Tawrah) and the criterion (of right and wrong) so that you may be guided aright.

Musa was on Mount At-Tur for a period of 40 days during which he was given the Tablets and the Tawrah to guide the people between right and wrong, between good and bad. His people, however, were up to mischief and instead committed a major transgression, an act of Shirk, by making a gold calf which they began worshipping.

The person who made the calf was a man by the name of As-Samiri[li]; he used the ornaments that the Israelites had borrowed from the Copts (before departing Egypt under the cover of the night, the Israelites took the things that they had borrowed from the Copts). In addition, just before Fir'awn drowned, Jibril had appeared and enticed Fir'awn's horse into the sea; at this point, As-Samiri had taken dust from the horse that Jibril was riding. After As-Samiri had made the calf from the ornaments, he then threw the dust on the calf. As soon as he threw the dust, the calf made a mooing sound.

When the Israelites heard this, they began dancing around the calf and showered it with blessings; soon they fell in love with the calf and began worshipping it.

The children of Israel kill each other in repentance

2.54   **And (remember) when Musa said to his people: "O my people! Verily, you have wronged yourselves by worshipping the calf. So turn in repentance to your Creator and kill yourselves (the innocent kill the wrongdoers among you), that will be better for you with your Creator." Then He accepted your repentance. Truly, He is the One Who accepts repentance, the Most Merciful.**

When the Children of Israel realized the error of their ways, they repented to Allah. Musa, through the guidance of Allah, commanded them to kill wrongdoers among them, as is described in the following hadith:

> *"Allah ordered Musa to command his people to kill each other. He ordered those who worshipped the calf to sit down and those who did not worship the calf to stand holding knives in their hands. When they started killing them, a great darkness suddenly overcame them. After the darkness lifted, they had killed seventy thousand of them. Those who were killed among them were forgiven, and those who remained alive were also forgiven."*[lii]

The children of Israel ask to see Allah

2.55 **And (remember) when you said: "O Musa! We shall never believe in you till we see Allah plainly." But you were seized with a thunderbolt (lightning) while you were looking.**

2.56 **Then We raised you up after your death, so that you might be grateful.**

No sooner had the Children of Israel earned Allah's forgiveness, some of them continued in their transgression by asking to see Allah. When Musa presented the Tablets to them he said: "These Tablets have Allah's Book, containing what He commanded you and what He forbade for you." They replied: "Should we believe this statement because you said it? By Allah, we will not believe until we see Allah in the open, until He shows us Himself and says: This is my book, therefore, adhere to it. Why does He not talk to us as He talked to you, O Musa?'"

These people numbered no fewer than 70 men and they were struck by a thunderbolt. When Musa pleaded with Allah for their forgiveness, Allah informed him that these 70 men had worshipped the calf. In His benevolence, Allah brought them back to life whilst the others were watching so that they might be grateful.

The Shade, the Manna and the Quail

2.57 **And We shaded you with clouds and sent down on you Al-Manna and the quail, (saying): "Eat of the good lawful things We have provided for you," (but they rebelled). And they did not wrong Us but they wronged themselves.**

The clouds referred to in the above verse were white and provided shade for the Israelites, protecting them from the sun's heat. It was stated that the clouds were cooler and better than the type we see today[liii].

The Al-Manna has been described as follows:

> *"The manna, which was whiter than milk and sweeter than honey, used to rain down on the Children of Israel, just as the snow falls, from dawn until sunrise. One of them would collect enough for that particular day, for if it remained more than that, it would spoil. On the sixth day, Friday, one would collect enough for the sixth and the seventh day, which was the Sabbath during which one would not leave home to seek his livelihood, or for anything else. All this occurred in the wilderness."[liv]*

The Salwa was a bird that looked like a quail[lv]; it was stated that the Salwa is a bird in Paradise about the size of a sparrow[lvi]. It has been further described as follows:

> *"The Salwa is a bird that is similar to a sparrow. During that time, an Israelite could catch as many quails as was sufficient for that particular day, otherwise the meat would spoil. On the sixth day, Friday, he would collect what is enough for the sixth and seventh day, the Sabbath, during which one was not allowed to depart his home to seek anything."[lvii]*

The Jews enter the town proud and arrogant

2.58 And (remember) when We said: "Enter this town (Jerusalem) and eat bountifully therein with pleasure and delight wherever you wish, and enter the gate in prostration (or bowing with humility) and say: 'Forgive us,' and We shall forgive you your sins and shall increase (reward) for the good-doers."

2.59 But those who did wrong changed the word from that which had been told to them for another, so We sent upon the wrong-doers Rijz (a punishment) from the heaven because of their rebelling against Allah's Obedience.

After hundreds of years of tyranny, Allah rescued the Children of Israel from the Fir'awn. Allah now commanded Musa to command the Israelites to return to Jerusalem and to fight the disbelieving 'Amaliq (Canaanites) who were dwelling in the holy land at that time. Allah was commanding them to perform Jihad. But the Israelites refused and made one excuse after another, saying they were tired and that the 'Amaliq were too strong physically and they could not prevail over them. The Qur'an describes this exchange in more detail in Surah 5, Verses 20 to 26.

Due to their refusal to obey Allah to perform Jihad to expel the disbelievers from the holy land, Allah sent them wandering into the wilderness for a period of 40 years; they wandered in the land of At-Tih and Allah ensured that they kept wandering from one area to another, unable to find their way out.

Musa passed away during the 40 years of wandering. Once these years were complete, and under the command of Yushua bin Nun (known as Joshua in the Bible and Tawrah) the Children of Israel finally performed Jihad and Allah gave them victory.

When they entered the city victorious, they were commanded by Allah to do so with humility for it was Allah who gave them victory. However, the people rebelled and entered the city with pride and arrogance, with their heads raised high in defiance.

They were commanded to say 'Hittah', which means 'relieve us from our errors and sins'. But they were haughty and mocked this command and said 'Hintah', which means 'grain seed'.

As is stated in several Verses of the Qur'an, they did not mock Allah but they mocked themselves; by disobeying and transgressing the limits ordained by Allah, Allah sent down his Rijz, meaning His punishment.

The twelve springs

2.60   **And (remember) when Musa asked for water for his people, We said: "Strike the stone with your stick." Then gushed forth therefrom twelve springs. Each (group of) people knew its own place for water. "Eat and drink of that which Allah has provided and do not act corruptly, making mischief on the earth."**

The above Verse has been explained as follows:

> *"The Children of Israel had a square stone that Musa was commanded to strike with his staff and, as a result, twelve springs burst out of that stone, three on each side. Each tribe was, therefore, designated a certain spring, and they used to drink from their springs. They never had to travel from their area, they would find the same bounty in the same manner they had in the first area."*[lviii]

At the time of Musa, there were 12 tribes amongst the Children of Israel, and each tribe took water that was assigned to them.

The children of Israel ask for inferior foods than what Allah had blessed them with and are covered in humiliation

2.61   **And (remember) when you said: "O Musa! We cannot endure one kind of food. So invoke your Lord for us to bring forth for us of what the earth grows, its herbs, its cucumbers, its Fum (wheat or garlic), its lentils and its onions." He said: "Would you exchange that which is better for that which is lower? Go you down to any town and you shall find what you want!" And they were covered with humiliation and misery, and they drew on themselves the Wrath of Allah. That was because they used to disbelieve the Ayat (proofs, evidences, verses, lessons, signs, revelations, etc.) of Allah and killed the Prophets wrongfully. That was because they disobeyed and used to transgress the bounds (in their disobedience to Allah, i.e. commit crimes and sins).**

When the Children of Israel asked for different foods, Musa stated that what they sought was easy for it was available in every town; however, what Allah had blessed them with was given to them and them alone.

As a result of their ungratefulness the Children of Israel were covered in humiliation and misery and they deserved the Wrath of Allah which they had earned by disobeying the Almighty and killing the Messengers and Prophets that Allah had blessed them with. In reference to this, Prophet Muhammad [PBUH] said:

> *"The people who will receive the most torment on the Day of Resurrection are: a man who was killed by a Prophet or who killed a Prophet, an unjust ruler and one who mutilates (the dead)."[lix]*

Believing in Allah and performing righteous deeds

> **2.62   Verily! Those who believe and those who are Jews and Christians, and Sabians, whoever believes in Allah and the Last Day and do righteous good deeds shall have their reward with their Lord, on them shall be no fear, nor shall they grieve.**

Before Prophet Muhammad [PBUH] was sent, each of the peoples who followed the Prophet that was sent to them were on the right path. However, when Allah sent Prophet Muhammad [PBUH], he is to be followed. For any good deed to be accepted from anyone by Allah, it must be in accordance with the Qur'an and conform to the Sunnah of Prophet Muhammad [PBUH]; if it does not, no good deed will be accepted[lx].

Why were the Jews called Yahud? Yahud means to repent because they repented when they disobeyed Allah and He sent down His Wrath on them. It is also stated that they were called Yahud because they were the children of Prophet Ya'qub's eldest son, Yahuda (known in the Bible and Tawrah as Judah).

Why were the Christians called Nasara? Because they gave aid and support to one another; it has also been said that they inhabited a land called An-Nasirah (known in the Bible as Nazareth).

Who were the Sabians? The Sabians did not follow a specific religion and they lived according to their Fitrah (meaning their instinct and nature).

Allah takes the Covenant from the Jews

2.63   **And (O Children of Israel, remember) when We took your covenant and We raised above you the Mount (saying): "Hold fast to that which We have given you, and remember that which is therein so that you may acquire Taqwa.**

2.64   **Then after that you turned away. Had it not been for the Grace and Mercy of Allah upon you, indeed you would have been among the losers.**

The mount that Allah raised above the Children of Israel was At-Tur – this is explained further in surah 7, Verse 171.

When Allah commanded them to hold fast to what they were given, this means that they were commanded to read and obey the Tawrah[lxi], which was given to them via Prophet Musa. However, even after giving the pledge to Allah that they would, the Children of Israel back-tracked and broke their pledge.

The Jews breach the Sabbath

2.65   **And indeed you knew those amongst you who transgressed in the matter of the Sabbath (i.e. Saturday). We said to them: "Be you monkeys, despised and rejected."**

2.66   **So We made this punishment an example for those in front of it and those behind it, and a lesson for Al-Muttaqin (the pious).**

How the Jews breached the sanctity of the Sabbath is described as follows: the Jews in the town used to deceit to circumvent the Sabbath; they were commanded not to carry out any business activities or cooking / hunting etc on Saturday (the Sabbath) as is written in the Tawrah. However, when they fished, they placed nets out on the water before the day of the Sabbath and when the fish were caught on Saturday, they would go in the night to collected the fish. Hence, they disobeyed Allah's command as was stated in the Tawrah, which they pledged to adhere to.

When they did that, Allah changed these people into monkeys (it was also said that the young people were turned into monkeys whilst the older ones were turned into swine)[lxii]. It has also been described that: "These people were turned into howling monkeys with tails, after being men and women."[lxiii]

The people who were turned into monkeys (and swine) only lived on the earth for three days before they died – they did not eat nor did they drink and nor did they have offspring. Hence, they are not the monkeys and swines that exist today for Allah created them and everything else in the universe in the six days of creation.

What is meant by 'for those in front of it and those behind it' is that these people who were transformed into monkeys and swines was an example for surrounding villages, and by preserving their story in the Qur'an, they are an example to people throughout the ages who defy the commands of Allah.

The murdered Israeli man and the cow

The story of the murdered Israeli man has been described as follows: "There was a man from among the Children of Israel who was impotent. He had substantial wealth, and only a nephew who would inherit from him. So his nephew killed him and moved his body at night, placing it at the doorstep of a certain man. The next morning, the nephew cried out for revenge, and the people took up their weapons and almost fought each other. The wise men among them said: "Why would you kill each other, while the Messenger of Allah is still among you?" So they went to Musa and mentioned the matter to him; the next verse describes what Musa said to them[lxiv]:

> **2.67**   **And (remember) when Musa said to his people: "Verily, Allah commands you that you slaughter a cow." They said: "Do you make fun of us?" He said: "I take Allah's Refuge from being among Al-Jahilin (the ignorant or the foolish)."**

However, the Children of Israel then began to dispute with Musa as to what type of cow it should be.

> **2.68**   **They said: "Call upon your Lord for us that He may make plain to us what it is!" He said: "He says, 'Verily, it is a cow neither too old nor too young, but (it is) between the two conditions', so do what you are commanded."**

> **2.69**   **They said: "Call upon your Lord for us to make plain to us its color." He said: "He says, 'It is a yellow cow, bright in its color, pleasing to the beholders.'"**

> **2.70**   **They said: "Call upon your Lord for us to make plain to us what it is. Verily to us all cows are alike, And surely, if Allah wills, we will be guided."**

> **2.71**   **He (Musa) said: "He says, 'It is a cow neither trained to till the soil nor water the fields, sound, having no blemish in it.'" They said: "Now you have brought the truth." So they slaughtered it though they were near to not doing it.**

This story has been further described as follows: "Had they not disputed, it would have been sufficient for them to slaughter any cow. However, they disputed, and the matter was made more difficult for them, until they ended up looking for the specific cow that they were later ordered to slaughter. They found the designated cow with a man. He said: 'By Allah! I will only sell it for its skin's fill of gold.' So they paid the cow's fill of its skin in gold and slaughtered it."[lxv]

2.72   And (remember) when you killed a man and fell into dispute among yourselves as to the crime. But Allah brought forth that which you were hiding.

2.73   So We said: "Strike him (the dead man) with a piece of it (the cow)." Thus Allah brings the dead to life and shows you His Ayat (proofs, evidences, verses, lessons, signs, revelations, etc.) so that you may understand.

The story concludes as follows: "They touched the dead man with a part of it. He stood up, and they asked him: 'Who killed you?' He said: 'That man,' and pointed to his nephew. He died again, and his nephew was not allowed to inherit from him. Thereafter, whoever committed murder for the purpose of gaining inheritance was not allowed to inherit."[lxvi]

Allah also states in the last Verse above that resurrection will occur and this was yet again directly shown to the Jews so that they believe in the Almighty.

In fact, there are no few than five instances in Surah Al-Baqarah alone that directly attribute the Power of Allah to bring the dead back to life.

Harshness of the Jews and inanimate object

2.74   **Then, after that, your hearts were hardened and became as stones or even worse in hardness. And indeed, there are stones out of which rivers gush forth, and indeed, there are of them (stones), which split asunder so that water flows from them, and indeed, there are of them (stones), which fall down for fear of Allah. And Allah is not unaware of what you do.**

The above Verse testifies to the fact that that the hearts of the Children of Israel, despite witnessing tremendous miracles and being saved from destruction and ruin by Allah time and time again, became harder than stones. They were never going to believe and this has been confirmed by their rejection of Prophet 'Isa whom they conspired with the Romans to try and kill and also their rejection of Prophet Muhammad [PBUH].

The above Verse also testifies that solid inanimate objects possess a certain degree of awareness; this has been confirmed by Prophet Muhammad [PBUH] in several hadiths including the following:

> *"This (Mount Uhud) is a mount that loves us and that we love."*[lxvii]

> *"I know a stone in Makkah that used to greet me with the Salam before I was sent. I recognize this stone now."*[lxviii]

> *"On the Day of Resurrection it (meaning the Black Stone) will testify for those who kiss it."*[lxix]

We will discuss this in more detail in Surah 41, Verse 21.

The Jews at the time of Prophet Muhammad (PBUH) were never going to believe in him

2.75   **Do you (faithful believers) covet that they will believe in your religion in spite of the fact that a party of them (Jewish rabbis) used to hear the Word of Allah (the Tawrah), then they used to change it knowingly after they understood it?**

2.76   **And when they (Jews) meet those who believe (Muslims), they say: "We believe", but when they meet one another in private, they say: "Shall you (Jews) tell them (Muslims) what Allah has revealed to you [about the description of Prophet Muhammad [PBUH], that they (Muslims) may argue with you (Jews) about it before your Lord?" Have you (Jews) then no understanding?**

2.77   **Know they (Jews) not that Allah knows what they conceal and what they reveal?**

The above Verses refer to the deviant sect of Jews whose fathers saw the incredible miracles and Power of Allah but who then defied the commands of the Almighty. It has been stated that: "They are the Jews who used to hear Allah's Words and then alter them after they understood and comprehended them."[lxx] It has also been said that: "Those who used to alter it and conceal its truths; they were their scholars."[lxxi]

How the Jewish rabbis changed the word of Allah has been described as follows: "They altered the Tawrah that Allah revealed to them, making it say that the lawful is unlawful and the prohibited is allowed, and that what is right is false and that what is false is right. So when a person seeking the truth comes to them with a bribe, they judge his case by the Book of Allah, but when a person comes to them seeking to do evil with a bribe, they take out the other (distorted) book, in which it is stated that he is in the right. When someone comes to them who is not seeking what is right, nor offering them bribe, then they enjoin righteousness on him."[lxxii]

The Jews rejected Prophet Muhammad [PBUH] even though it was written in their Tawrah; indeed, it has been said: "They believe that Muhammad [PBUH] is the Messenger of Allah, but he was only sent for you Arabs."[lxxiii] But when they met each other, they would say: "Do not convey the news about this Prophet to the Arabs, because you used to ask Allah to grant you victory over them but when he came he was sent to them and not you."

Hence, the Jews of the time of Prophet Muhammad [PBUH] used to invoke Allah to send them a Messenger so that they could defeat the Arabs and in fact they would boast to the Arabs that when he came, they would destroy the Arabs. However, when Allah sent the Final Messenger, he was not one of them but was an Arab. Indeed, it is up to Allah whom He sends as His Messenger. We will discuss this in more detail in due course.

Another group of Jews distort the Book of Allah

2.78   And there are among them (Jews) 'Ummyyun (unlettered) people, who know not the Book, but they trust upon Amani (false desires) and they but guess.

2.79   Then woe to those who write the Book with their own hands and then say: "This is from Allah," to purchase with it a little price! Woe to them for what their hands have written and woe to them for that they earn thereby.

This is another group of the Jews, not their rabbis, who were uneducated in the Holy Books, who doctored them for a small price, meaning they sold them for small worldly gain. However, Allah responds to the actions of these Jews with the word: "Waylun", meaning, 'woe'; and hence the above Verse warns these Jews of utter destruction for what they have done.

The Jews think they will be in the Fire for only a few days

2.80 **And they (Jews) say: "The Fire shall not touch us but for a few numbered days." Say (O Muhammad Peace be upon him to them): "Have you taken a covenant from Allah, so that Allah will not break His Covenant? Or is it that you say of Allah what you know not?"**

Following the conquest of Khaybar, when the Jews tried to kill Prophet Muhammad [PBUH] by serving him a poisoned sheep, the Prophet [PBUH] asked them a question:

""Who are the people of the (Hell) Fire?" They said: "We shall remain in the (Hell) Fire for a short period, and after that you will replace us in it." The Prophet [PBUH] said: "May you be cursed and humiliated in it! By Allah, we shall never replace you in it.""[lxxiv]

Those who commit sins will enter the Fire

2.81   **Yes! Whosoever earns evil and his sin has surrounded him, they are dwellers of the Fire (i.e. Hell); they will dwell therein forever.**

2.82   **And those who believe and do righteous good deeds, they are dwellers of Paradise, they will dwell therein forever.**

Allah states that whoever commits evil and sin and continues in evil and sin will enter the Fire and will remain there forever. Where it says: 'his sin has surrounded him', this means: "Whoever dies before repenting from his wrongs."[lxxv]

In order to avoid the major sins, particularly that of Shirk (polytheism), it is important to be mindful of the small sins; Prophet Muhammad [PBUH] elaborated on this as follows:

> *"Beware of the belittled sins, because they gather on a person until they destroy him."*[lxxvi]

With regards to those who perform righteous deeds and worship Allah in accordance with the Qur'an and the Sunnah of Prophet Muhammad [PBUH], Allah has promised that they will enter Paradise and will abide therein forever.

The Rights of Allah and the people

2.83   **And (remember) when We took a covenant from the Children of Israel, (saying): Worship none but Allah (Alone) and be dutiful and good to parents, and to kindred, and to orphans and Al-Masakin (the poor), and speak good to people and perform As-Salat and give Zakat. Then you slid back, except a few of you, while you are backsliders.**

Allah commanded the Children of Israel to worship Him and Him Alone, which is the highest and most important right, that of Allah, followed by the rights of the creatures. Of the creatures, the first and foremost right is that of the parents; in fact, Allah has mentioned the rights of one's parents along with His rights in many Verse of the Qur'an.

How important the rights of parents are has been described in the following hadith narrated by Ibn Mas'ud:

> *"I said: "O Messenger of Allah! What is the best deed?" He said: "Performing the prayer on time." I said: "Then what?" He said: "Being kind to one's parents." I said: "Then what?" He said: "Jihad in the cause of Allah."*[lxxvii]

The next rights belong to relatives followed by orphans and then the Al-Masakin (meaning the poor) (whom we will discuss in more detail in Surah 4).

After commanding the people to be kind to one another, Allah then commanded them to say good words to them and hence this covers the two parts of manners, good speech and good actions. Prophet Muhammad [PBUH] added:

> *"Do not belittle any form of righteousness, and even if you did not find any good deed except meeting your brother with a smiling face, then do so."*[lxxviii]

The Jews breach the Covenant

2.84   And (remember) when We took your covenant (saying): Shed not the blood of your people, nor turn out your own people from their dwellings. Then, (this) you ratified and (to this) you bore witness.

2.85   After this, it is you who kill one another and drive out a party of you from their homes, assist (their enemies) against them, in sin and transgression. And if they come to you as captives, you ransom them, although their expulsion was forbidden to you. Then do you believe in a part of the Scripture and reject the rest? Then what is the recompense of those who do so among you, except disgrace in the life of this world, and on the Day of Resurrection they shall be consigned to the most grievous torment. And Allah is not unaware of what you do.

2.86   Those are they who have bought the life of this world at the price of the Hereafter. Their torment shall not be lightened nor shall they be helped.

The above Verses are in reference to the Jews during the time when the Prophet Muhammad [PBUH] and the early Muslims had migrated to Madinah. In Madinah, there were two Arab tribes and three Jewish tribes – two of the Jewish tribes were allied to one Arab tribe and the third Jewish tribe was allied to the other Arab tribe. When war broke out, the Jewish tribes ally themselves with their respective Arab tribes and fight against other Jewish tribes, even though they were commanded in the Tawrah not to fight each other. They would kill other Jews and would loot whatever they could from the defeated Jewish tribe. And as the above Verses state, when hostilities ended between the various parties, they would then implement the Tawrah by releasing their prisoners. This is why Allah stated in the above Verse: "Then do you believe in a part of the Scripture and reject the rest?" As a result of this, the Jews cannot and must not be entrusted to convey what was revealed in the Tawrah that was given to Musa as they omitted things they did not like and added what their hearts desired. They changed the Word of Allah for the sake of this world.

The Jews denied and killed the Messengers of Allah

2.87   **And indeed, We gave Musa the Book and followed him up with a succession of Messengers. And We gave 'Isa, the son of Maryam, clear signs and supported him with Ruh-il-Qudus. Is it that whenever there came to you a Messenger with what you yourselves desired not, you grew arrogant? Some you disbelieved and some you killed.**

Allah states that He sent Musa with the Tawrah and followed him with several other Messengers, including 'Isa (known in the Bible as Jesus) and supported him with Ruh-il-Qudus (meaning the angel Jibril). Each of the Messengers after Musa upheld what was written in the Tawrah, particularly the parts that the Jews had changed, hence they became even more rebellious towards these Messengers; some they disbelieved and some they killed.

The Jews even tried to kill the Prophet Muhammad [PBUH] as he stated:

> *"I kept feeling the effect of what I ate (from the poisoned sheep) during the day of Khaybar, until now, when it is the time that the aorta will be cut off (meaning when death is near)."*[lxxix]

The Jews proclaim that they do not understand nor need Allah's Message

2.88   **And they say: "Our hearts are Ghulf (i.e. do not hear or understand Allah's Word)." Nay, Allah has cursed them for their disbelief, so little is that which they believe.**

The Jews stated that their hearts are Ghulf, meaning their hearts are screened[lxxx] and they do not understand[lxxxi]. Others have stated that they meant: "Our hearts contain every type of knowledge and do not need the knowledge that you (O Muhammad [PBUH]) have."[lxxxii]

The Jews were expecting Prophet Muhammad (PBUH) but then arrogantly rejected him

> **2.89**   And when there came to them (the Jews), a Book (this Qur'an) from Allah confirming what is with them (the Tawrah) and the Injil (Gospel)], although aforetime they had invoked Allah (for the coming of Muhammad [PBUH]) in order to gain victory over those who disbelieved, then when there came to them that which they had recognized, they disbelieved in it. So let the Curse of Allah be on the disbelievers.

Before Prophet Muhammad [PBUH] was sent, the Jews used to invoke Allah to send the Prophet that was mentioned in their Tawrah, so that they could overpower the Arab tribes of Aws and Khazraj of Madinah. However, when Allah sent Prophet Muhammad [PBUH], they rejected him because he was sent from amongst the Arabs and not amongst the Jews. They omitted all reference to Prophet Muhammad [PBUH] from the Tawrah so that none of their people would believe in the Prophet Muhammad [PBUH] and hope that others too would reject him. However, Allah cursed them for their rejection of Prophet Muhammad [PBUH] and disbelief in the Message that Allah had sent.

> **2.90**   How bad is that for which they have sold their ownselves, that they should disbelieve in that which Allah has revealed (the Qur'an), grudging that Allah should reveal of His Grace unto whom He will of His slaves. So they have drawn on themselves wrath upon wrath. And for the disbelievers, there is disgracing torment.

The Jews were so arrogant that: "Allah became angry with them because of their disbelief in the Injil and 'Isa and He became angry with them again, because they disbelieved in Muhammad [PBUH] and the Qur'an."[lxxxiii]

Regarding arrogance, Prophet Muhammad [PBUH] said:

> *"The arrogant people will be gathered on the Day of Resurrection in the size of ants, but in the shape of men. Everything shall be above them, because of the humiliation placed on them, until they enter a prison in Jahannam called 'Bawlas' where the fire will surround them from above. They shall drink from the puss of the people of the Fire."*[lxxxiv]

The Jews claim they are believers, yet it was they who killed the Prophets

2.91   And when it is said to them (the Jews): "Believe in what Allah has sent down," they say: "We believe in what was sent down to us." And they disbelieve in that which came after it, while it is the truth confirming what is with them. Say (O Muhammad [PBUH] to them): "Why then have you killed the Prophets of Allah aforetime, if you indeed have been believers?"

2.92   And indeed Musa came to you with clear proofs, yet you worshipped the calf after he left, and you were Zalimun (polytheists and wrong-doers).

Allah states that although the Jews claimed to be believers, they refused to believe in the prophets and instead killed some of them. As for those Jews who claimed to follow Musa, when he left to go to the meeting place with Allah on Mount Tur, they worshipped the calf in his absence. And they refused to believe in the Prophets that were sent after Musa.

2.93   And (remember) when We took your covenant and We raised above you the Mount (saying): "Hold firmly to what We have given you and hear (Our Word)". They said: "We have heard and disobeyed." And their hearts absorbed (the worship of) the calf because of their disbelief. Say: "Worst indeed is that which your faith enjoins on you if you are believers."

The above Verse means that Allah raised Mount Tur above them so that they were compelled to believe and agreed to Allah's Covenant. However, it was not long before they disbelieved when they worshipped the calf. And their greatest sin was when they disbelieved in the Final and the Greatest of all the Messengers, Muhammad [PBUH], so how can they then claim to be believers.

The Jews are challenged to invoke Allah to destroy the unjust party

2.94 Say to (them): "If the home of the Hereafter with Allah is indeed for you specially and not for others, of mankind, then long for death if you are truthful."

2.95 But they will never long for it because of what their hands have sent before them (i.e. what they have done). And Allah is All-Aware of the Zalimin (polytheists and wrong-doers).

2.96 And verily, you will find them (the Jews) the greediest of mankind for life and (even greedier) than those who ascribe partners to Allah. One of them wishes that he could be given a life of a thousand years. But the grant of such life will not save him even a little from (due) punishment. And Allah is All-Seer of what they do.

The Jews claim that they are the chosen people and they will not suffer on the Day of Resurrection or some claim that they will only suffer a little compared to others. Allah then commanded Prophet Muhammad [PBUH] to say to them: "Invoke Allah to bring death to the lying camp among the two (either the Muslims or the Jews)."[lxxxv] The Jews turned down the challenge of Prophet Muhammad [PBUH]; "had the Jews invoked Allah for death, they would have perished."[lxxxvi] It has also been stated that not a single Jew would have remained alive on the earth if they had accepted the challenge.

The reason why the Jews did not accept the challenge was because they are fully aware of what they have done, how they have changed Allah's Words in the Books, how they have killed the Prophets, and how they will end up in the Hellfire on the Day of Resurrection. As a result of this, the Jews in particular and the disbelievers in general want to live for as long as possible. It has been stated that "the Jews are most eager for this life. They wish they could live for a thousand years. However, living for a thousand years will not save them from torment, just as Iblis' long life did not benefit him, due to being a disbeliever."[lxxxvii]

The Jews are the enemies of Jibril

2.97 Say (O Muhammad [PBUH]): "Whoever is an enemy to Jibril (Gabriel) (let him die in his fury), for indeed he has brought it (this Qur'an) down to your heart by Allah's Permission, confirming what came before it [i.e. the Tawrah and the Injil] and guidance and glad tidings for the believers.

2.98 "Whoever is an enemy to Allah, His Angels, His Messengers, Jibril and Mika'il, then verily, Allah is an enemy to the disbelievers."

"The above Verses were revealed in response to the Jews who claimed that Jibril is an enemy of the Jews and that Mika'il is their friend."[lxxxviii]

To highlight how one of the leaders amongst the Jews became a Muslim as a direct result of the revelation from Jibril to Prophet Muhammad [PBUH], we quote the following hadith:

"When `Abdullah bin Salam heard the arrival of the Prophet [PBUH] at Madinah, he came to him and said: "I am going to ask you about three things which nobody knows except a prophet: What is the first portent of the Hour? What will be the first meal taken by the people of Paradise? Why does a child resemble its father, and why does it resemble its maternal uncle."

Allah's Messenger [PBUH] said: "Jibril has just now told me of their answers."

`Abdullah said: "He (i.e. Jibril), from amongst all the angels, is the enemy of the Jews."

Allah's Messenger [PBUH] said: "The first portent of the Hour will be a fire that will bring together the people from the east to the west; the first meal of the people of Paradise will be extra-lobe (caudate lobe) of fish-liver. As for the resemblance of the child to its parents: If a man has sexual intercourse with his wife and gets discharge first, the child will resemble the father, and if the woman gets discharge first, the child will resemble her."

On that `Abdullah bin Salam said: "I testify that you are the Apostle of Allah."

`Abdullah bin Salam further said: "O Allah's Messenger [PBUH]! The Jews are liars, and if they should come to know about my conversion to Islam before you ask them (about me), they would tell a lie about me."

The Jews came to Allah's Messenger [PBUH] and `Abdullah went inside the house. Allah's Apostle asked (the Jews): "What kind of man is `Abdullah bin Salam amongst you?"

They replied: "He is the most learned person amongst us, and the best amongst us, and the son of the best amongst us."

Allah's Messenger [PBUH] said: "What do you think if he embraces Islam (will you do as he does)?"

The Jews said: "May Allah save him from it."

Then `Abdullah bin Salam came out in front of them saying: "I testify that None has the right to be worshipped but Allah and that Muhammad is the Apostle of Allah."

Thereupon they said: "He is the evilest among us, and the son of the evilest amongst us," and continued talking badly of him.

Allah has stated that if anyone is an enemy to Allah, to any of His Prophets, any of his angels, and in particular Jibril or Mika'il, then Allah will be an enemy to that person. Indeed, Prophet Muhammad [PBUH] said:

"Allah said: "Whoever takes a friend of Mine as an enemy, will have started a war with Me.""[lxxxix]

The Jews abandoned the Book of Allah and practiced magic

2.99 And indeed We have sent down to you manifest Ayat and none disbelieve in them but Fasiqun (those who rebel against Allah's Command).

2.100 Is it not (the case) that every time they make a covenant, some party among them throw it aside? Nay! (the truth is) most of them believe not.

2.101 And when there came to them a Messenger from Allah (i.e. Muhammad [PBUH]) confirming what was with them, a party of those who were given the Scripture threw away the Book of Allah behind their backs as if they did not know!

2.102 They followed what the Shayatin (devils) gave out (falsely of the magic) in the lifetime of Sulayman (Solomon). Sulayman did not disbelieve, but the Shayatin (devils) disbelieved, teaching men magic and such things that came down at Babylon to the two angels, Harut and Marut, but neither of these two (angels) taught anyone (such things) till they had said: "We are only for trial, so disbelieve not (by learning this magic from us)." And from these (angels) people learn that by which they cause separation between man and his wife, but they could not thus harm anyone except by Allah's Leave. And they learn that which harms them and profits them not. And indeed they knew that the buyers of it (magic) would have no share in the Hereafter. And how bad indeed was that for which they sold their own selves, if they but knew.

2.103 And if they had believed and guarded themselves from evil and kept their duty to Allah, far better would have been the reward from their Lord, if they but knew!

When Allah sent Prophet Muhammad [PBUH] to the people He reminded the Jews of the covenant that He had with them, to believe in the Messenger when he was sent. However, the Jews then proclaimed: "By Allah! Allah never made a covenant with us about Muhammad, nor did He take a pledge from us at all." That is why Allah stated in the above Verse: "Is it not (the case) that every time they make a covenant, some party among them throw it aside."[xc] It has also been said that: "There is not a promise that they make, but they break it and abandon it. They make a promise today and break it tomorrow."[xci]

When Prophet Muhammad [PBUH] came with the Qur'an, which confirmed what was in the Tawrah, they disputed with him. This has been described as follows: "When Muhammad [PBUH] came to them, they wanted to contradict with him using the Tawrah. However, the Tawrah and the Qur'an affirmed each other. So the Jews gave up on using the Tawrah, and took to the Book of Asaf (this the name of the Book revealed to the Prophet Sulayman), and the magic of Harut and Marut, which indeed did not conform to the Qur'an."[xcii]

Prophet Sulayman did not practice magic

The Jews claimed that Prophet Sulayman practiced magic and he was a sorcerer, one of their many lies against the Prophets of Allah. This story is worth retelling in detail.

Well before the time of Prophet Sulayman, the devils would ascend to the heavens and eavesdrop on the conversations between the angels about what would occur on the earth. The devils would return to the earth and convey what they had heard to soothsayers. The soothsayers would then tell the people for a fee. At that stage, everything the devils told the soothsayers was true, and hence the people began to believe the soothsayers. However, the devils then began to tell lies to the soothsayers, so much so that they told seventy lies for every truth. The Children of Israel believed and told the people that the Jinns know the matters of the Unseen, an attribute only applicable to Allah. The people then recorded these words in books.

When Prophet Sulayman was sent, he took these books and buried them under his throne and stated that if anyone said that the devils know matters of the Unseen, he would chop off his head. When Prophet Sulayman passed away and the righteous followers of his time perished, a new generation came after them. To these people Shaytan appeared in the form of a man and guided them to the treasure which was buried under the throne of Prophet Sulayman. When they dug the treasure out and found the books, Shaytan said to them that Prophet Sulayman (whom Allah had granted leadership over every soul on the earth, including humans and animals and birds and even the jinn) controlled these souls with the magic contained in the books. As a result, the Children of Israel spread false rumors that Prophet Sulayman was a magician and a sorcerer.

When Prophet Muhammad [PBUH] was sent, the Jews then began to argue with him using the Books that Prophet Sulayman had buried, Books that they had kept all these years.

The above Verse states that the two angels, Harut and Marut, did not teach the people magic unless they believed that they were testing them. This has been described as follows: "When a man would come to the two angels they would advise him: "Do not fall into disbelief. We are a test." When the man would ignore their advice, they would say: "Go to that pile of ashes and urinate on it." When he would urinate on the ashes, a light, meaning the light of faith, would depart from him and would shine until it entered heaven. Then something black that appeared to be smoke would descend and enter his ears and the rest of his body, and this is Allah's anger. When he told the angels what happened, they would teach him magic."[xciii]

With regards to practicing magic, this is strictly prohibited in Islam: "Whoever came to a soothsayer or a sorcerer and believed in what he said, will have disbelieved in what Allah revealed to Muhammad [PBUH]."[xciv]

The evil work of Shaytan and the magic that results in separation between a husband and a wife has been explained by Prophet Muhammad [PBUH] who said:

"Iblis erects his throne on water and sends his emissaries among the people. The closest person to him is the person who causes the most Fitnah. One of them (a devil) would come to him and would say: "I kept inciting so-and-so, until he said such and such words." Iblis would say: "No, by Allah, you have not done much." Another devil would come to him and would say: "I kept inciting so-and-so, until I separated between him and his wife." Iblis would draw him closer and embrace him, saying: "Yes, you did well." "[xcv]

What the above hadith means that the whispers of the devils would result in one spouse thinking and believing the other is either ugly or ill-mannered, and will continue to find faults with the other until they separate.

Do not imitate the disbelievers

2.104 O you who believe! Say not (to the Messenger [PBUH]) Ra'ina but say Unzurna (Do make us understand) and hear. And for the disbelievers there is a painful torment.

2.105 Neither those who disbelieve among the people of the Scripture (Jews and Christians) nor Al-Mushrikin (the idolaters) like that there should be sent down unto you any good from your Lord. But Allah chooses for His Mercy whom He wills. And Allah is the Owner of Great Bounty.

The word Ra'ina means 'hear us' in Arabic but is an insult in the Hebrew language. This is the word that the Children of Israel would use to the Prophet Muhammad [PBUH], may Allah curse them; and this is why Allah forbade this practice for the believers and instead use the word Unzurna.

The Children of Israel are very devious and would use trickery in their words to confuse the people. As an example, when greeting the Muslims, they would say: "As-Samu 'alaykum" which means 'death be to you'. And when they did this, the Muslims were commanded to answer with the words: "Wa 'alaykum" which means 'and to you too'.

In addition to the above, the Muslims are encouraged not to follow the disbelievers in any way, whether in their acts of worship, their religious festivals, their speech, their dress code, and anything that has not been ordained by the Qur'an and the Sunnah of Prophet Muhammad [PBUH]. Indeed, Prophet Muhammad [PBUH] said:

> *"Whoever imitates a people is one of them."*[xcvi]

The above Verse also highlights the extreme enmity that the disbelievers have for the Muslims and we are encouraged to several all friendship with them.

Abrogation occurs even though the Jews deny it

2.106   **Whatever a Verse (revelation) do Nansakh (We abrogate) or Nunsiha (cause to be forgotten), We bring a better one or similar to it. Know you not that Allah is able to do all things?**

2.107   **Know you not that it is Allah to Whom belongs the dominion of the heavens and the earth? And besides Allah you have neither any Wali (protector or guardian) nor any helper.**

Abrogation of Verses and laws is another miracle of the Qur'an and is something that the Jews deny. There are many examples of abrogation. For example, Allah permitted Adam to marry his sons to his daughters as they were the first of mankind, but later this was prohibited; when Nuh and the believers disembarked the Ark, they were permitted to eat all types of foods, but later some foods were made off-limits; Israel and his children were permitted to be married to two sisters at one time, but later this was prohibited in the Tawrah. There are many more examples of abrogation in the Qur'an.

Believers are refrained from asking unnecessary questions

2.108 **Or do you want to ask your Messenger (Muhammad [PBUH]) as Musa was asked before (i.e. show us openly our Lord?) And he who changes faith for disbelief, verily, he has gone astray from the right way.**

During the time of Prophet Muhammad [PBUH] the Muslims were commanded not to ask questions that would ultimately make it difficult for them to follows Islam. An example of this is as follows:

The Prophet [PBUH] told the Companions that Allah had ordered them to perform Hajj. A man asked: "Every year, O Messenger of Allah?" The Prophet [PBUH] did not answer him, but he repeated his question three times. Then the Prophet [PBUH] said: "No. Had I said yes, it would have been ordained, and you would not have been able to implement it."[xcvii]

Prohibition of following the people of the book

2.109   **Many of the people of the Scripture (Jews and Christians) wish that if they could turn you away as disbelievers after you have believed, out of envy from their own selves, even after the truth (that Muhammad [PBUH] is Allah's Messenger) has become manifest unto them. But forgive and overlook, till Allah brings His Command. Verily, Allah is Able to do all things.**

2.110   **And perform the Salah and give Zakah, and whatever of good you send forth for yourselves before you, you shall find it with Allah. Certainly, Allah is the Seer of what you do.**

The Jews and Christians want the Muslims to give up their faith but Allah instructed them to avoid their practices and to forgive them. However, this Verse was abrogated by Surah 9, Verse 5 which states: "Then kill the Mushrikin wherever you find them" and Surah 9, Verse 29 which states: "Fight against those who believe not in Allah, nor in the Last Day."

After instructing the believers to avoid the practices of the Jews and Christians, Allah commands the believers to perform acts of worship, especially the Salah and Zakah, and to know that Allah is fully aware of everything that a person does.

The false desires of the Jews and Christians

2.111   And they say: "None shall enter Paradise unless he be a Jew or a Christian." These are their own desires. Say (O Muhammad [PBUH]), "Produce your Burhan (proof) if you are truthful."

2.112   Yes! But whoever submits his face (himself) to Allah (i.e. follows Allah's Religion of Islamic Monotheism) and he is a Muhsin then his reward is with his Lord (Allah), on such shall be no fear, nor shall they grieve.

2.113   The Jews said that the Christians follow nothing (i.e. are not on the right religion); and the Christians said that the Jews follow nothing (i.e. are not on the right religion); though they both recite the Scripture. Like unto their word, said those (the pagans) who know not. Allah will judge between them on the Day of Resurrection about that wherein they have been differing.

For a good deed to be accepted by Allah it must meet two conditions: the deed must be only for the sake of Allah and it must be in accordance with the Shari'ah. If either of these is not met, then it will be rejected. For example, if it is done for the sake of Allah but does not conform to the Shari'ah, then it will be rejected. Also, if the deed is in accordance with the Shari'ah outwardly but was not for the sake of Allah, then it will also be rejected.

The above Verse also states how the Jews and Christians dispute with each other; the Jews state that 'Isa was not a Prophet, even though this was written in the Tawrah given to Musa and the Jews gave their pledge to believe and support 'Isa when he was sent. The Christians claim that Musa was not a Prophet and was not given the Tawrah, yet this is what is written in the Injil that was given to 'Isa. Hence, each party disputes with each other, citing the Books that they have themselves doctored to meet their own false desires.

Those who prevent the believers from entering the Masjids

2.114   **And who is more unjust than those who forbid that Allah's Name be mentioned (i.e. prayers and invocations) in Allah's Masjids and strive for their ruin? It was not fitting that such should themselves enter them (Allah's Masjids) except in fear. For them there is disgrace in this world, and they will have a great torment in the Hereafter.**

The above Verse relates to the Quraysh idolaters who prevented Prophet Muhammad [PBUH] and the believers from entering Makkah from Al-Hudaybiyyah. Allah states that those who prevent people from the Masjids will face great torment in the Hereafter.

Allah also states in Surah 9, Verse 18: "The Masjids of Allah shall be maintained only by those who believe in Allah and the Last Day; perform the Salah and give Zakah and fear none but Allah. It is they who are on true guidance."

Allah has also stated that disbelievers are not permitted to enter Masjids except to satisfy the terms of an armistice or a treaty.

Facing the Qiblah

2.115   **And to Allah belong the east and the west, so wherever you turn (yourselves or your faces) there is the Face of Allah (and He is High above, over His Throne). Surely! Allah is All-Sufficient (for His creatures' needs), Knowing.**

This was the first part of the Qur'an that was abrogated.

When he lived in Makkah, Prophet Muhammad [PBUH] performed his Salah in the direction of Bayt Al-Maqdis (the Qiblah at the time) with the Kaabah in between him and the Qiblah. When the Prophet [PBUH] migrated to Madinah, he continued to pray towards Bayt Al-Maqdis until Allah revealed the above Verses, upon which he changed his prayer direction towards the Kaabah, the new Qiblah.

How long did the Prophet [PBUH] pray towards Bayt Al-Maqdis until the above Verse was revealed? The sources vary from 10 months up to 17 months. Allah knows best!

Refuting the claim that Allah has begotten a son

2.116 **And they (Jews, Christians and pagans) say: Allah has begotten a son (children or offspring). Glory be to Him (Exalted be He above all that they associate with Him). Nay, to Him belongs all that is in the heavens and on earth, and all are Qanitun (bound in servitude) to Him.**

2.117 **The Originator of the heavens and the earth. When He decrees a matter, He only says to it: "Be!" – and it is.**

Allah Created everything and has complete Power over everything; He sustains everything and provides for everything. Each and every single creature is His servant and they are all owned by Him. How then can the Creator of everything have a child? This is one of the highest grades of Shirk (polytheist, associating others in partnership with Allah) and anyone who makes such a claim will end up in the deepest depths of Hell.

The above Verse provides the explanation that Allah Created the Heavens and the earth, and every minute detail contained therein, in six days; when He decrees something to happen, all He has to do is to say, 'Be' and it is.

2.118 **And those who have no knowledge say: "Why does not Allah speak to us (face to face) or why does not a sign come to us?" So said the people before them words of similar import. Their hearts are alike, We have indeed made plain the signs for people who believe with certainty.**

When the disbelievers among the Quraysh and the disbelievers among the people of the Book (Jews and Christians) said to the Prophet Muhammad [PBUH] why Allah does not speak to them, Allah stated that the disbelievers throughout history have made the same claim, even those who witnessed tremendous miracles by the Will of Allah. They disbelieved and will continue to disbelieve irrespective of the evidences before them.

2.119 **Verily, We have sent you (O Muhammad [PBUH]) with the truth (Islam), a bringer of glad tidings (for those who believe in what you brought, that they will enter Paradise) and a warner (for those who disbelieve in what you brought, they will enter the Hell-fire). And you will not be asked about the dwellers of the blazing Fire.**

Allah confirms that He sent Prophet Muhammad [PBUH] to bring glad tidings to those who believe and warn those who disbelieve.

The prohibitions of trying to please the Jews and Christians

2.120   Never will the Jews nor the Christians be pleased with you (O Muhammad [PBUH]) till you follow their religion. Say: "Verily, the Guidance of Allah (i.e. Islamic Monotheism) that is the (only) guidance. And if you (O Muhammad [PBUH]) were to follow their (Jews and Christians) desires after what you have received of Knowledge (i.e. the Qur'an), then you would have against Allah neither any Wali (protector or guardian) nor any helper.

2.121   Those to whom We gave the Book recite it as it should be recited (Yatlunahu Haqqa Tilawatihi) they are the ones that believe therein. And whoso disbelieve in it (the Qur'an), those are they who are the losers.

The above Verses guide the Muslims to know that whatever they do will never please the Jews and Christians until you abandon the religion of Islam and follow them, hence the Muslims should not try to please them; however, Muslims should do all they can to please Allah for only He is worthy of worship.

The correct meaning of those who recite the Book as it should be recited (Yatlunahu Haqqa Tilawatihi) is: "They are those who when they recite an Ayah that mentions mercy, they ask Allah for it, and when they recite an Ayah that mentions torment, they seek refuge with Allah from it."[xcviii]

2.122   O Children of Israel! Remember My Favor which I bestowed upon you and that I preferred you over the 'Alamin (mankind and jinns) (of your time).

2.123   And fear the Day (of Judgment) when no person shall avail another, nor shall compensation be accepted from him, nor shall intercession be of use to him, nor shall they be helped.

Ibrahim was an Imam for the people

2.124   **And (remember) when the Lord of Ibrahim (Abraham) tried him with (certain) commands, which he fulfilled. He (Allah) said (to him): "Verily, I am going to make you an Imam (a leader) of mankind (to follow you)." (Ibrahim) said: "And of my offspring (to make leaders)." (Allah) said: "My covenant (Prophethood) includes not Zalimin (polytheists and wrong-doers)."**

The above Verse highlights the honor that Allah gave Ibrahim for Allah made him an Imam (meaning a leader) amongst the people. His conduct was exemplary and he carried out the Commands of Allah without hesitation; as a result, Allah Commanded the people to follow him.

When Ibrahim asked Allah to grant his offspring to become leaders, Allah replied that He would not include the polytheists and wrongdoers among his offspring. However, all the Prophets that came after Ibrahim were from his offspring as is stated in Surah 29, Verse 27: "And We ordained among his offspring Prophethood and the Book."

In addition, "the unjust person does not qualify to be a Khalifah, a ruler, one who gives religious verdicts, a witness or even a narrator (of hadiths)."[xcix]

The Maqam and purifying the Kaabah

2.125 **And (remember) when We made the House (the Ka'bah at Makkah) a place of resort for mankind and a place of safety. And take you (people) the Maqam (place) of Ibrahim [or the stone on which Ibrahim stood while he was building the Ka'bah] as a place of prayer (for some of your prayers, e.g. two Rak'at after the Tawaf of the Ka'bah at Makkah), and We commanded Ibrahim and Isma'il (Ishmael) that they should purify My House (the Ka'bah at Makkah) for those who are circumambulating it, or staying (I'tikaf), or bowing or prostrating themselves (there, in prayer).**

The Kaabah at Makkah is a place of safety, meaning "safe from enemies and armed conflict. During the time of Jahiliyyah, the people were often victims of raids and kidnapping, while the people in the area surrounding it were safe and not subject to kidnapping."[c] It is also said that "whoever enters it shall be safe."[ci]

What is the Maqam, also known as the Station of Ibrahim?

When they were building the Kaabah, Ibrahim stood on a particular stone so that he could raise the walls higher on each side, whilst his son Isma'il was passing him the stones; the particular stone that Ibrahim stood on became known as Maqam.

As is stated in the above Verse, the believers were instructed to pray next to it. How this came about has been described as follows: "When the Prophet Muhammad [PBUH] performed Tawaf, 'Umar bin Al-Khattab asked him: "Is this the Maqam of our father?" He said: "Yes." 'Umar said: "Should be take it a place of prayer?" So Allah revealed: "And take you (people) the Maqam (place) of Ibrahim as a place of prayer.""[cii]

Although the Maqam used to be situated right next to the House, it was moved during the reign of 'Umar bin Al-Khattab (the second Caliph after Abu Bakr of the Four Rightly Guided Caliphs) farther to the east so that those who go around the House in Tawaf are able to perform it easily, without disturbing those who are praying next to the Maqam.

Regarding the first two of the Four Rightly Guided Caliphs, the Prophet Muhammad [PBUH] said:

> *"Imitate the two men who will come after me: Abu Bakr and 'Umar."*[ciii]

The final part of the above Verse commands the people to purify the masjids from all impurities.

Makkah is a Sacred City

2.126   And (remember) when Ibrahim said: "My Lord, make this city (Makkah) a place of security and provide its people with fruits, such of them as believe in Allah and the Last Day." He (Allah) answered: "As for him who disbelieves, I shall leave him in contentment for a while, then I shall compel him to the torment of the Fire, and worst indeed is that destination!"

Makkah is a city that is a sanctuary; Prophet Muhammad [PBUH] said:

"Allah has made this city a sanctuary (sacred place) the Day He created the heavens and earth. Therefore, it is a sanctuary until the Day of Resurrection because Allah made it a sanctuary. It was not legal for anyone to fight in it before me, and it was legal for me for a few hours of one day. Therefore, it is a sanctuary until the Day of Resurrection, because Allah made it a sanctuary. None is allowed to uproot its thorny shrubs, or to chase its game, or to pick up something that has fallen, except by a person who announces it publicly, nor should any of its trees be cut." Al-'Abbas said: "O Messenger of Allah! Except the lemon-grass, for our goldsmiths and for our graves." The Prophet added: "Except lemon-grass."[civ]

It has also been recorded that "no one is allowed to carry weapons in Makkah."[cv]

And when Ibrahim asked Allah to provide sustenance to the believers in the city, Allah stated that He would grant sustenance to both the believers and the disbelievers who are in the city, but in the next life, the disbelievers will taste the torment of the Fire.

Performing a good deed and asking Allah to accept the good deed

2.127 **And (remember) when Ibrahim and (his son) Isma'il were raising the foundations of the House (the Ka'bah at Makkah), (saying): "Our Lord! Accept (this service) from us. Verily, You are the Hearer, the Knower."**

2.128 **"Our Lord! And make us submissive unto You and of our offspring a nation submissive unto You, and show us our Manasik (all the ceremonies of pilgrimage - Hajj and 'Umrah, etc.), and accept our repentance. Truly, You are the One Who accepts repentance, the Most Merciful.**

When Ibrahim and his son Isma'il were building the Kaabah, they were performing a very great and noble deed. However, whilst they were building the Kaabah they were also invoking Allah to accept their deeds. This is the behavior of the sincere believers, for while they carry out noble and great deeds, they are still fearful that Allah will not accept it from them.

The Story of the Kaabah

This has been described in a long and famous hadith, which provides knowledge of the Kaabah, the rites of Hajj and a dutiful wife; we will quote it in its entirety.[cvi]

> *"Prophet Ibrahim took Isma'il and his mother and went away with them until he reached the area of the House, where he left them next to a tree above Zamzam in the upper area of the Masjid. During that time, Isma'il's mother was still nursing him. Makkah was then uninhabited, and there was no water source in it. Ibrahim left them there with a bag containing some dates and a water-skin containing water. Ibrahim then started to leave, and Isma'il's mother followed him and said, 'O Ibrahim! To whom are you leaving us in this barren valley that is not inhabited?' She repeated the question several times and Ibrahim did not reply. She asked, 'Has Allah commanded you to do this?' He said, 'Yes.' She said, 'I am satisfied that Allah will never abandon us.' Ibrahim left, and when he was far enough away where they could not see him, close to Thaniyyah, he faced the House, raised his hands and supplicated to Allah:*

> **"O our Lord! I have made some of my offspring to dwell in an uncultivable valley by Your Sacred House (meaning the Ka'bah at Makkah); in order, O our Lord, that they may perform As-Salat (Iqamat-as-Salat), so fill some hearts among men with love towards them, and O Allah provide them with fruits so that they may give thanks." [14:37]**

> *Isma'il's mother then returned to her place, started drinking water from the water-skin and nursing Isma'il. When the water was used up, she and her son became*

thirsty. She looked at him, and he was suffering from thirst; she left, because she disliked seeing his face in that condition. She found the nearest mountain to where she was, As-Safa, ascended it and looking, in vain, hoping to see somebody. When she came down to the valley, she raised her garment and ran, just as a tired person runs, until she reached the Al-Marwah mountain. In vain, she looked to see if there was someone there. She ran to and fro (between the two mountains) seven times."

This is the reason why the people make the trip between As-Safa and Al-Marwah during Hajj and Umrah.

"When she reached Al-Marwah, she heard a voice and said, 'Shush,' to herself. She tried to hear the voice again and when she did, she said, 'I have heard you. Do you have relief?' She found the angel digging with his heel (or his wing) where Zamzam now exists, and the water gushed out. Isma'il's mother was astonished and started digging, using her hand to transfer water to the water-skin.

Isma'il's mother started drinking the water and her milk increased for her child. The angel Jibril said to her, 'Do not fear abandonment. There shall be a House for Allah built here by this boy and his father. Allah does not abandon His people.' During that time, the area of the House was raised above ground level and the floods used to reach its right and left sides.

Afterwards some people of the tribe of Jurhum, passing through Kada', made camp at the bottom of the valley. They saw some birds, they were astonished, and said, 'Birds can only be found at a place where there is water. We did not notice before that this valley had water.' They sent a scout or two who searched the area, found the water, and returned to inform them about it. Then they all went to Isma'il's mother, next to the water, and said, 'O Mother of Isma'il! Will you allow us to be with you (or dwell with you)?' She said, 'Yes. But you will have no exclusive right to the water here.' They said, 'We agree.'

And thus they stayed there and sent for their relatives to join them.

Later on, her boy reached the age of puberty and married a lady from them, for Isma'il learned Arabic from them, and they liked the way he was raised. Isma'il's mother died after that.

Then an idea occurred to Ibrahim to visit his dependents. So he left (to Makkah). When he arrived, he did not find Ism'ail, so he asked his wife about him. She said, 'He has gone out hunting.' When he asked her about their living conditions, she complained to him that they live in misery and poverty. Ibrahim said (to her), 'When your husband comes, convey my greeting and tell him to change the threshold of his gate.' When Isma'il came, he sensed that they had a visitor and asked his wife, 'Did we have a visitor?' She said, 'Yes. An old man came to visit us and asked me about you, and I told him where you were. He also asked about our condition, and I told him that we live in hardship and poverty.' Isma'il said, 'Did he ask you to do anything?' She said, 'Yes. He asked me to convey his greeting and that you should change the threshold of your gate.' Isma'il said to her, 'He was my father and you are the threshold, so go to your family (i.e. you are divorced).' So he divorced her and married another woman.

The reason why Ibrahim [AS] ordered Isma'il [AS] to divorce his wife was because she was not subservient to Allah nor was she thankful to Allah for what He had provided her with nor was she dutiful to her husband.

We now move on to the part where Isma'il [AS] had remarried and Ibrahim [AS] again travelled to Makkah to meet with his son.

Again Ibrahim thought of visiting his dependents whom he had left (at Makkah). Ibrahim came to Isma'il's house, but did not find Isma'il and asked his wife, 'Where is Isma'il?' Isma'il's wife replied, 'He has gone out hunting.' He asked her about their condition, and she said that they have a good life and praised Allah. Ibrahim asked, 'What is your food and what is your drink?' She replied, 'Our food is meat and our drink is water.' He said, 'O Allah! Bless their meat and their drink.'"

"Ibrahim said, 'When Isma'il comes back, convey my greeting to him and ask him to keep the threshold of his gate.' When Isma'il came back, he asked, 'Has anyone visited us.' She said, 'Yes. A good looking old man,' and she praised Ibrahim, 'And he asked me about our livelihood and I told him that we live in good conditions.' He asked, 'Did he ask you to convey any message?' She said, 'Yes. He conveyed his greeting to you and said that you should keep the threshold of your gate.' Isma'il said, 'That was my father, and you are the threshold; he commanded me to keep you.'

On this occasion Ibrahim [AS] ordered his son to keep his wife for she praised Allah, was thankful for what He had given her, and was a dutiful wife. It is to be noted that those who do not live in Makkah cannot bear eating a diet only containing meat and water.

Ibrahim then came back visiting and found Isma'il behind the Zamzam well, next to a tree, mending his arrows. When he saw Ibrahim, he stood up and they greeted each other, just as the father and son greet each other. Ibrahim said, 'O Isma'il, Your Lord has ordered me to do something.' He said, 'Obey your Lord.' He asked Isma'il, 'Will you help me?' He said, 'Yes, I will help you.' Ibrahim said, 'Allah has commanded me to build a house for Him there,' and he pointed to an area that was above ground level. So, both of them rose and started to raise the foundations of the House. Ibrahim started building (the Ka'bah), while Isma'il continued handing him the stones. Both of them were saying, 'O our Lord! Accept (this service) from us. Verily, You are the Hearing, the Knowing.'

The Kaabah will be destroyed by an Ethiopian just before the Last Hour

Prophet Muhammad [PBUH] said:

"Dhus-Sawiqatayn (literally, a person with two lean legs) from Ethiopia will destroy the Kaabah and will loot its adornments and cover. It is as if I see him now: bald, with thin legs striking the Kaabah with his axe."[cvii]

Since Ibrahim asked Allah to grant his offspring the Prophethood after him, there is an important hadith regarding how one's offspring can benefit a person in the next life; Prophet Muhammad [PBUH] said:

"When the son of Adam dies, his deeds end except for three deeds: an ongoing charity, a knowledge that is being benefited from and a righteous son who supplicates (to Allah) for him."[cviii]

Ibrahim invokes Allah to send Muhammad [PBUH]

2.129 **"Our Lord! Send amongst them a Messenger of their own, who shall recite unto them Your Verses and instruct them in the Book (this Qur'an) and purify them. Verily, You are the Mighty, the Wise."**

Ibrahim was the first person to mention Prophet Muhammad [PBUH] to the people and since then, the Children of Israel knew that Allah would send a Prophet that the whole of mankind would follow. The last Prophet among the Children of Israel, 'Isa, mentioned the Prophet [PBUH] by name (as is stated in Surah 61, Verse 6).

Ibrahim practiced Islamic Monotheism and he should be followed

2.130 And who turns away from the religion of Ibrahim (i.e. Islamic Monotheism) except him who befools himself? Truly, We chose him in this world and verily, in the Hereafter he will be among the righteous.

2.131 When his Lord said to him: "Submit (i.e. be a Muslim)!" He said: "I have submitted myself (as a Muslim) to the Lord of the 'Alamin (mankind, jinns and all that exists)."

2.132 And this (submission to Allah, Islam) was enjoined by Ibrahim upon his sons and by Ya'qub (Jacob), (saying): "O my sons! Allah has chosen for you the (true) religion, then die not except as Muslims."

Ibrahim is mentioned in several Verses of the Qur'an as a role model, who practiced Islamic Monotheism, and how he should be followed. Whilst his people, including his father, were ardent and devout worshippers of idols, Ibrahim believed in Allah and carried out His Commands without hesitation.

Who was Ya'qub (known in the Tawrah and Bible as Jacob)? Ya'qub was a Prophet who built Bayt-ul-Maqdis, the mosque in Jerusalem. One of the Companions asked Prophet Muhammad [PBUH] about the masjids:

"I said: 'O Messenger of Allah [meaning Prophet Muhammad [PBUH]], which Masjid was the first to be built?' He said: "Al-Masjid Al-Haram." I said: "Then which?' He said: "Bayt Al-Maqdis." I said: "How long between them?" He said: "Forty years." [cix]

Ya'qub's will to his children

2.133   Or were you witnesses when death approached Ya'qub (Jacob)? When he said unto his sons: "What will you worship after me?" They said: "We shall worship your Ilah (God - Allah), the Ilah (God) of your fathers, Ibrahim, Isma'il, Ishaaq, One Ilah, and to Him we submit (in Islam)."

2.134   That was a nation who has passed away. They shall receive the reward of what they earned and you of what you earn. And you will not be asked of what they used to do.

Ya'qub's advice to his children was to worship Allah and Allah Alone. The reason why he deliberately and very carefully instructed his children was because on the Day of Resurrection, his children would not be able to call on him to help them. A hadith states:

"Whoever has slowed on account of his deeds will not get any faster on account of his family lineage."[cx]

The Jews and Christians ask Muhammad [PBUH] to follow them

2.135   **And they say: "Be Jews or Christians, then you will be guided." Say (to them, O Muhammad [PBUH]): "Nay, (we follow) only the religion of Ibrahim, Hanifa (Islamic Monotheism), and he was not of Al-Mushrikun (those who worshipped others along with Allah)."**

The above Verse was revealed when the Jews and Christians stated directly to Prophet Muhammad [PBUH] that he should become a Jew or a Christian respectively; however, Allah countered this by saying that the true believers are those who follow the religion of Ibrahim which was Islamic Monotheism and he was not a polytheist like the other religions.

The command to believe in all the prophets

2.136 **Say (O Muslims): "We believe in Allah and that which has been sent down to us and that which has been sent down to Ibrahim, Isma'il, Ishaaq, Ya'qub, and to Al-Asbat [the twelve sons of Ya'qub], and that which has been given to Musa and 'Isa, and that which has been given to the Prophets from their Lord. We make no distinction between any of them, and to Him we have submitted (in Islam)."**

The believers believe in all the Prophets and the Message that they brought and we should not believe the Jews or the Christians because they have distorted Allah's Books to meet their own false desires. It has been said:

> *"The people of the Book used to read the Tawrah in Hebrew and translate it into Arabic for the Muslims. The Messenger of Allah [PBUH] said: "Do not believe the People of the Book, nor reject what they say. Rather, say: 'We believe in Allah and in what was sent down to us.'"*[cxi]

As for the meaning of Al-Asbat, it means: "Al-Asbat are the twelve sons of Ya'qub (Jacob), and each one of them had an Ummah of people from his descendants. This is why they are called Al-Asbat."[cxii]

Allah's Sibghah is Islam

2.137   So if they believe in the like of that which you believe, then they are rightly guided; but if they turn away, then they are only in opposition. So Allah will suffice for you against them. And He is the All-Hearer, the All-Knower.

2.138   [Our Sibghah (religion) is] the Sibghah of Allah (Islam) and which Sibghah can be better than Allah's? And we are His worshippers.

The previous prophets were not Jews or Christians

2.139   Say (O Muhammad [PBUH] to the Jews and Christians): "Dispute you with us about Allah while He is our Lord and your Lord? And we are to be rewarded for our deeds and you for your deeds. And we are sincere to Him in worship and obedience (i.e. we worship Him Alone and none else, and we obey His Orders)."

2.140   Or say you that Ibrahim, Isma'il, Ishaaq, Ya'qub and Al-Asbat [the twelve sons of Ya'qub] were Jews or Christians? Say: "Do you know better or does Allah? And who is more unjust than he who conceals the testimony he has from Allah? And Allah is not unaware of what you do."

2.141   That was a nation who has passed away. They shall receive the reward of what they earned, and you of what you earn. And you will not be asked of what they used to do.

The leaders and scholars amongst the Jews and Christians were the worst amongst them. It has been said: "They used to recite the Book of Allah He sent to them that stated that the true religion is Islam and that Muhammad [PBUH] is the Messenger of Allah. Their Book also stated that Ibrahim, Isma'il, Ishaaq, Ya'qub and the tribes were neither Jews nor Christians. They testified to these facts, yet hid them from the people. This is why Allah said: "And Allah is not unaware of what you do."[cxiii]

Changing the Qiblah

2.142   **The fools (idolaters, hypocrites and Jews) among the people will say: "What has turned them (Muslims) from their Qiblah [prayer direction (towards Jerusalem)] to which they used to face in prayer." Say: (O Muhammad [PBUH]): "To Allah belong both, east and the west. He guides whom He wills to a Straight Way."**

2.143   **Thus We have made you [true Muslims - real believers of Islamic Monotheism, true followers of Prophet Muhammad [PBUH] and his Sunnah (legal ways)], a Wasat (just and the best) nation, that you be witnesses over mankind and the Messenger (Muhammad [PBUH]) be a witness over you. And We made the Qiblah (prayer direction towards Jerusalem) which you used to face, only to test those who followed the Messenger (Muhammad [PBUH]) from those who would turn on their heels (i.e. disobey the Messenger [PBUH]). Indeed it was great (heavy and difficult) except for those whom Allah guided. And Allah would never make your faith (prayers) to be lost (i.e. your prayers offered towards Jerusalem). Truly, Allah is full of kindness, the Most Merciful towards mankind.**

2.144   **Verily! We have seen the turning of your (Muhammad's [PBUH]) face towards the heaven. Surely, We shall turn you to a Qiblah (prayer direction) that shall please you, so turn your face in the direction of Al-Masjid- al-Haram (at Makkah). And wheresoever you people are, turn your faces (in prayer) in that direction. Certainly, the people who were given the Scripture (i.e. Jews and Christians) know well that, that (your turning towards the direction of the Ka'bah at Makkah in prayers) is the truth from their Lord. And Allah is not unaware of what they do.**

Allah's Messenger [PBUH] used to offer prayers towards Bayt Al-Maqdis (in Jerusalem), but would keep looking at the sky awaiting Allah's command (to change the Qiblah) – that is when Allah revealed the above Verses which changed the direction of prayer.[cxiv]

The story of the change in the direction of the prayer (Qiblah) has been described in detail as follows: "Allah's Messenger [PBUH] offered his prayers facing Bayt Al-Maqdis (Jerusalem) for sixteen or seventeen months, but he wished that he could pray facing the Kaabah (at Makkah). The first prayer which he offered (facing the Kaabah) was the 'Asr (Afternoon) prayer in the company of some people. Then one of those who had offered that prayer with him, went out and passed by some people in a mosque who were in the bowing position (in Ruku') during their prayers (facing Jerusalem). He addressed them saying: 'By Allah, I bear witness that I have offered prayer with the Prophet [PBUH] facing Makkah.' Hearing that, those people immediately changed their direction towards the House (Kaabah) while still as they were (i.e. in the same bowing position)."[cxv]

Whilst the Prophet Muhammad [PBUH] and the Muslims were facing Bayt Al-Maqdis during their prayers, the Jews were happy as it was the same direction as them. However, when Allah Commanded them to face the Kaabah, the Jews asked why they had changed their direction of prayer. Allah responded by saying that both the east and west belong to Him!

The above Verses confirm that all Muslims, whether living in the east, west, north or south, should face the Kaabah when offering their obligatory prayers. The exception to this rule is the Nafl (voluntary) prayer while one is travelling; in this scenario, a person may face in any direction whilst his or her heart are intending the Kaabah. Other exceptions are when the Muslims are in the heat of batter, and in this scenario, they are permitted to offer the prayer as best as he or she is able; another exception are those who offer the prayer in the wrong direction thinking it was right, and in this scenario they are forgiven because Allah does not burden a people beyond their means.

When one of the Companions asked Prophet Muhammad [PBUH] about the prayers that they had offered when facing Jerusalem before the Qiblah was changed, Allah stated: "And Allah would never make your prayers to be lost," meaning they were valid and would be accepted by Allah.

Allah also states in the above Verses that the Jews and Christians knew of the coming of Prophet Muhammad [PBUH] from their Books (before they began changing them) and in them it was stated that Prophet Muhammad [PBUH] would change the direction of the Qiblah. This is the reason why the Jews and Christians became intensely jealous when Allah Commanded Prophet Muhammad [PBUH] with the change in the direction of the Qiblah for they knew it was the truth from their Books. Prophet Muhammad [PBUH] said:

> "They do not envy us for a matter more than they envy us for Jumu'ah (Friday) to which Allah has guided us and from which they were led astray; for the (true) Qiblah to which Allah has directed us and from which they were led astray; and for our saying 'Amin' behind the Imam (leader of the prayer)."[cxvi]

The Ummah of Muhammad [PBUH] is a Wasat nation

The word Wasat means the just and best. It has been narrated that Prophet Muhammad [PBUH] said:

> "Nuh will be called on the Day of Resurrection and will be asked: 'Have you conveyed (the Message)?' He will say: 'Yes'. His people will be summoned and asked: 'Has Nuh conveyed (the Message) to you?' They will say: 'No warner came to us and no one (Prophet) was sent to us.' Nuh will be asked: 'Who testifies for you?' He will say: 'Muhammad and his Ummah'.
> This is why Allah said: "Thus We have made you a Wasat nation."
> The Prophet [PBUH] said: "The Wasat means the 'Adl (just). You will be summoned to testify that Nuh has conveyed (his Message), and I will attest to your testimony."[cxvii]

The high importance of the Ummah of Prophet Muhammad [PBUH] and the testimony of each person has been highlighted in a hadith in which the Prophet Muhammad [PBUH] responded to the Companions:

> ""Any Muslim for whom four testify that he was righteous, then Allah will enter him into Paradise." We said: "What about three?" He said: "And three." We said: "And two?" He said: "And two." We did not ask him about (the testimony) of one (believing) person."[cxviii]

The Jews and Christians will never follow Muhammad's [PBUH] Qiblah

2.145 And even if you were to bring to the people of the Scripture (Jews and Christians) all the Ayat (proofs, evidences, verses, lessons, signs, revelations, etc.), they would not follow your Qiblah (prayer direction), nor are you going to follow their Qiblah. And they will not follow each other's Qiblah. Verily, if you follow their desires after that which you have received of knowledge (from Allah), then indeed you will be one of the Zalimin (polytheists, wrong-doers, etc.).

The Jews and Christians know the truth but hide it

2.146 Those to whom We gave the Scripture (Jews and Christians) recognize him (Muhammad [PBUH] or the Ka'bah at Makkah) as they recognize their sons. But verily, a party of them conceal the truth while they know it – [i.e. the qualities of Muhammad [PBUH] which are written in the Tawrah and the Injil].

2.147 (This is) the truth from your Lord. So be you not one of those who doubt.

Every nation has a Qiblah

2.148   **For every nation there is a direction to which they face (in their prayers). So hasten towards all that is good. Wheresoever you may be, Allah will bring you together (on the Day of Resurrection). Truly, Allah is Able to do all things.**

It has been stated that: "The Jew has a direction to which he faces (in the prayer). The Christian has a direction to which he faces. Allah has guided you, O (Muslim) Ummah, to a Qiblah which is the true Qiblah."[cxix]

Mentioning the change of Qiblah direction for the third time

2.149   And from wheresoever you start forth (for prayers), turn your face in the direction of Al-Masjid-al-Haram (at Makkah), that is indeed the truth from your Lord. And Allah is not unaware of what you do.

2.150   And from wheresoever you start forth (for prayers), turn your face in the direction of Al-Masjid-al-Haram (at Makkah), and wheresoever you are, turn your faces towards, it (when you pray) so that men may have no argument against you except those of them that are wrong-doers, so fear them not, but fear Me! - And so that I may complete My Blessings on you and that you may be guided.

Why was changing the Qiblah direction mentioned three times? Firstly, Allah agreed to what His Prophet [PBUH] has wished for; secondly, Allah confirmed that it was also the truth from Him; and thirdly, Allah refuted the claims of the Jews who asserted that the Prophet Muhammad [PBUH] face their direction of Qiblah, but when it was changed they knew it was the truth from Allah (as was stated in their Books), yet they rejected the Message and the Prophet [PBUH].

Allah sends Muhammad [PBUH] to bring His Message

2.151   **Similarly (to complete My Blessings on you) We have sent among you a Messenger (Muhammad [PBUH]) of your own, reciting to you Our Verses (the Qur'an) and purifying you, and teaching you the Book (the Qur'an) and the Hikmah (i.e. Sunnah, Islamic laws and Fiqh - jurisprudence), and teaching you that which you used not to know.**

2.152   **Therefore remember Me (by praying, glorifying). I will remember you, and be grateful to Me (for My countless favors on you) and never be ungrateful to Me.**

After stating that He sent Muhammad [PBUH] to bring His Message, Allah Commands the believers to remember and thank Him for the countless favors that He has bestowed on each and every single person and a result, the believers will be granted even greater rewards. Prophet Muhammad stated:

"Allah the Exalted said: "O son of Adam! If you mention Me to yourself, I will mention you to Myself. If you mention Me in a gathering, I will mention you in a gathering of the angels (or said in a better gathering). If you draw closer to Me by a hand span, I will draw closer to you by a forearm's length. If you draw closer to Me by a forearm's length, I will draw closer to you by an arm's length. And if you come to Me walking, I will come to you running.'"[cxx]

Patience and prayer

2.153   O you who believe! Seek help in patience and As-Salah (the prayer). Truly, Allah is with As-Sabirin (the patient).

The following hadith explains this Verse further:

"Amazing is the believer, for whatever Allah decrees for him, it is better for him! If he is tested with a bounty, he is grateful for it and this is better for him; and if he is afflicted with a hardship, he is patient with it and this is better for him."[cxxi]

With regard to patience (Sabr), this has been described as: "Sabr has two parts: patience for the sake of Allah concerning what He is pleased with (i.e. acts of worship and obedience), even if it is hard on the heart and the body; and patience when avoiding what He dislikes even if it is desired. Those who acquire these qualities will be among the patient persons whom Allah shall greet in the Hereafter."[cxxii]

The martyrs are not dead

2.154   And say not of those who are killed in the Way of Allah: "They are dead." Nay, they are living, but you perceive (it) not.

Those who are martyred for the sake of Allah are not dead but alive. In fact, the life of the martyrs has been described as follows:

"The souls of the martyrs are inside green birds and move about in Paradise wherever they wish. Then, they take refuge in lamps that are hanging under the Throne (of Allah). Your Lord looked at them and asked them: "What do you wish for?" They said: "What more could we wish for while You have favored us with what You have not favored any other of your creation?" He repeated the question again. When they realize that they will be asked (until they answer), they said: "We wish that You send us back to the earthly life, so that we fight in Your cause until we are killed in Your cause again," (because of what they enjoy of the rewards of martyrdom). The Lord then said: "I have written that they will not be returned to it (earthly life) again." "[cxxiii]

The believers are patient and will be rewarded

2.155 And certainly, We shall test you with something of fear, hunger, loss of wealth, lives and fruits, but give glad tidings to As-Sabirin (the patient).

2.156 Who, when afflicted with calamity, say: "Truly, to Allah we belong and truly, to Him we shall return."

2.157 They are those on whom are the Salawat (i.e. who are blessed and will be forgiven) from their Lord, and (they are those who) receive His Mercy, and it is they who are the guided ones.

When a calamity or an affliction strikes an individual, if he or she says: "Truly, to Allah we belong and truly, to Him we shall return," they will be rewarded because they are admitting that the return is to Allah.

Prophet Muhammad [PBUH] said:

"No Muslim is struck with an affliction and then says Istirja' when the affliction strikes, and then says: 'O Allah! Reward me for my loss and give me what is better than it,' but Allah will do just that."[cxxiv]

Umm Salamah remembered these words and when Umm Salamah lost her husband, she said: "O Allah! Compensate me for my loss and give me what is better than it." Not long afterwards, the Prophet Muhammad [PBUH] asked for her hand in marriage to which she agreed. She said: "Allah compensated me with who is better than Abu Salamah: Allah's Messenger [PBUH]."[cxxv]

Sa'i between As-Safa and Al-Marwah

2.158 **Verily, As-Safa and Al-Marwah (two mountains in Makkah) are of the Symbols of Allah. So it is not a sin on him who perform Hajj or 'Umrah (pilgrimage) of the House (the Ka'bah at Makkah) to perform (Tawaf) between them. And whoever does good voluntarily, then verily, Allah is All-Recognizer, All-Knower.**

The reason why the above Verse states 'it is not a sin' to perform Tawaf between As-Safa and Al-Marwah was because of the following: "Isaf (an idol) was on As-Safa while Na'ilah (another idol) was on Al-Marwah, and they used to touch (or kiss) them. After Islam came, they were hesitant about performing Tawaf between them. Thereafter the above Verse was revealed."[cxxvi]

Regarding the actual Tawaf, a hadith states: "Allah's Messenger [PBUH] finished the Tawaf around the House, and then went back to the Rukn (pillar, i.e. the Black Stone) and kissed it. He then went out from the door near As-Safa while reciting: 'Verily, As-Safa and Al-Marwah are of the symbols of Allah.' The Prophet [PBUH] then said: 'I start with what Allah has commanded me to start with [meaning start with Sa'i (i.e. fast walking) from the As-Safa."[cxxvii]

Those who hide religious commandments will be cursed forever

2.159 Verily, those who conceal the clear proofs, evidences and the guidance, which We have sent down, after We have made it clear for the people in the Book, they are the ones cursed by Allah and cursed by the cursers.

2.160 Except those who repent and do righteous deeds, and openly declare (the truth which they concealed). These, I will accept their repentance. And I am the One Who accepts repentance, the Most Merciful.

2.161 Verily, those who disbelieve, and die while they are disbelievers, it is they on whom is the Curse of Allah and of the angels and of mankind, combined.

2.162 They will abide therein (under the curse in Hell), their punishment will neither be lightened nor will they be reprieved.

The above Verses "were revealed about the People of the Scripture who hid the description of Muhammad [PBUH]."[cxxviii]

Regarding keeping knowledge from the people, Prophet Muhammad [PBUH] stated:

"Whoever was asked about knowledge that one has, but he hid it, then a bridle made of fire will be tied around his mouth on the Day of Resurrection."[cxxix]

Regarding cursing, it is lawful to curse the disbelievers; it is stated that 'Umar bin Al-Khattab and others who followed him used to curse the disbelievers during their prayers and outside prayers.

Allah's Greatest Name

2.163   **And your Ilah (God) is One Ilah (God - Allah), La ilaha illa Huwa (there is none who has the right to be worshipped but He), the Most Beneficent, the Most Merciful.**

In this Verse, Allah states that He is the only god, He has no partners nor any equals. He is Allah, the One, the Sustainer. And He is Ar-Rahman (the Most Beneficent) and Ar-Rahim (the Most Merciful) – we explained these two names in Surah Al-Fatihah.

The Prophet Muhammad [PBUH] said:

> "Allah's Greatest Name is contained in these two Ayat,"[cxxx] meaning in Verse 2.163 and 3.1 and 3.2.

The proofs for Tawhid

2.164   **Verily, in the creation of the heavens and the earth, and in the alternation of night and day, and the ships which sail through the sea with that which is of use to mankind, and the water (rain) which Allah sends down from the sky and makes the earth alive therewith after its death, and the moving (living) creatures of all kinds that He has scattered therein, and in the veering of winds and clouds which are held between the sky and the earth, are indeed Ayat (proofs, evidences, signs, etc.) for people of understanding.**

Allah states that it is He who Created everything, and if one comprehends the creation around oneself, one can only be amazed at how perfect and beautiful it is.

The night alters with the day, and even though the nights get longer during the winter, they never fail to follow the day, and vice versa. The sea is vast and Allah has made it strong enough to carry huge ships, some of which weigh tens of thousands of tons of steel, hence Allah has made mankind masters of the sea. Allah sends down rain from the sky to provide irrigation for the crops and for water for His creatures. And Allah has scattered people across the world, some of whom live far from the sea, yet He has Created hillocks and valleys and ravines that enable the water to course through to these people and animals. And the creatures are of all shapes and sizes, various colors and various characteristics, and also various uses for mankind and the habitats that they live and maintain. And by the 'veering of winds' this means that the wind sometimes brings mercy from the heat and humidity, and sometimes brings torment that ravages the surrounding areas. And the clouds are maintained by Allah and move according to the Will of Allah between the sky and the earth.

If one looks hard enough at the Creation of the Almighty, and how each element of it is maintained in its own system, particularly if one travels the vast areas of the earth, one cannot but be amazed at the Perfection of the Almighty.

The polytheists will face torment in this life and the Hereafter

2.165 **And of mankind are some who take (for worship) others besides Allah as rivals (to Allah). They love them as they love Allah. But those who believe, love Allah more (than anything else). If only, those who do wrong could see, when they will see the torment, that all power belongs to Allah and that Allah is severe in punishment.**

2.166 **When those who were followed disown (declare themselves innocent of) those who followed (them), and they see the torment, then all their relations will be cut off from them.**

2.167 **And those who followed will say: "If only we had one more chance to return (to the worldly life), we would disown (declare ourselves as innocent from) them as they have disowned (declared themselves as innocent from) us." Thus Allah will show them their deeds as regrets for them. And they will never get out of the Fire.**

Prophet Muhammad [PBUH] was asked what is the greatest sin – he replied:

"To appoint a rival to Allah while He Alone has created you."[cxxxi]

Allah has warned the disbelievers throughout the Qur'an that they will face severe punishment in the next life because of their associating others in worship than Allah. And as for those whom they worshipped, some of these disbelievers worshipped certain prophets whilst some worshipped angels; however, when the Prophets and angels state that at no stage did they ever say to anyone that they be worshipped instead of Allah, the disbelievers will plead with Allah to return back on to the earth and would not worship the Prophets or the angels. However, by then it will be too late and they will end up in the Hellfire.

We have stated in a previous hadith: "on the Day of Resurrection Allah will say to a servant: "Have I not allowed you to marry, honored you, made the horses and camels subservient to you and allowed you to become a chief and a master" He will say: "Yes." Allah will say: "Did you have Zann (meaning think) that you will meet Me?" He will say: "No." Allah will say: "This Day, I will forget you, just as you forgot Me.""[cxxxii]

As for those who worshipped idols that they had crafted with their own hands, they will see these idols in the Hellfire when they are thrown in.

May Allah save us from the Fire and grant us into Paradise.

Command to eat only lawful things and prohibition of following Shaytan

2.168   O mankind! Eat of that which is lawful and good on the earth, and follow not the footsteps of Shaytan (Satan). Verily, he is to you an open enemy.

2.169   He (Shaytan) commands you only what is evil and Fahsha (sinful), and that you should say about Allah what you know not.

Allah states that He has permitted the people to eat the pure and lawful things that He has granted them that do not cause harm to either the body or the mind. And it is the work of Shaytan when a person disregards this command and eats something that is prohibited; the exact meaning of "and follow not the footsteps of Shaytan" is: "Every act of disobedience to Allah is among the footsteps of Shaytan."[cxxxiii]

It has also been said that: "Any vow or oath that one makes while angry, is among the footsteps of Shaytan and its expiation is that of the vow (meaning feeding ten poor persons, clothing them, freeing a servant, or fasting three days – see Surah 5, Verse 89)."[cxxxiv]

The polytheists are just like animals in their belief

2.170 When it is said to them: "Follow what Allah has sent down." They say: "Nay! We shall follow what we found our fathers following." (Would they do that!) even though their fathers did not understand anything nor were they guided?

2.171 And the example of those who disbelieve is as that of him who shouts to the (flock of sheep) that hear nothing but calls and cries. (They are) deaf, dumb and blind. So they do not understand.

The above Verses were revealed regarding a group of Jews whom the Prophet Muhammad [PBUH] called to Islam; however, they replied that they would rather follow in their footsteps of their fathers. This is the response of the majority of disbelievers.

Allah states that the disbelievers are deaf (meaning they cannot hear the Message), dumb (meaning they cannot utter words that will benefit them) and blind (meaning they cannot recognize the true path to Allah).

Command to eat pure things and what is not permitted

2.172   **O you who believe (in the Oneness of Allah - Islamic Monotheism)! Eat of the lawful things that We have provided you with, and be grateful to Allah, if it is indeed He Whom you worship.**

2.173   **He has forbidden you only the Maitah (dead animals), and blood, and the flesh of swine, and that which is slaughtered as a sacrifice for others than Allah. But if one is forced by necessity without willful disobedience nor transgressing due limits, then there is no sin on him. Truly, Allah is Oft-Forgiving, Most Merciful.**

One of the acts of obedience to Allah is to eat only what He, the Creator and Sustainer of everything, has permitted to eat (and be thankful for what He has provided) and to refrain from eating those things that He has prohibited.

What has Allah prohibited from eating? Maitah means dead animals which have died prior to being slaughtered and these are prohibited. Excluded from this are dead animals from the sea; Prophet Muhammad [PBUH] said:

"Its water is pure and its dead are permissible."[cxxxv]

Allah has also prohibited eating something that has not been slaughtered as a sacrifice in Allah's Name. When the Prophet Muhammad's [PBUH] wife was asked about if one attends a feast in which there was meat which was not slaughtered in Allah's Name, she replied: "Do not eat from what has been slaughtered for that day, but eat from their vegetables."[cxxxvi]

Allah also prohibited eating the meat of swine, whether slaughtered in Allah's Name or not.

Prophet Muhammad [PBUH] also added:

"We have been allowed two dead things and two bloody things: fish and locusts; and liver and spleen."[cxxxvii]

Allah also commands the people that if they have no other option then they are commanded to eat those things that are prohibited; what this means is that otherwise they would die, or they would have to resort to other acts of disobedience such as robbery, rising up against their rulers etc. In these scenarios, there is no sin on the individual.

It has also been stated that "whoever is in dire need, but does not eat or drink until he dies, he will enter the Fire."[cxxxviii] What this means is that if one is in dire need, it is not just permissible but required to consume food, of whatever type, to stay alive.

Those who conceal what Allah has revealed for worldly gain

2.174 Verily, those who conceal what Allah has sent down of the Book, and purchase a small gain therewith (of worldly things), they eat into their bellies nothing but fire. Allah will not speak to them on the Day of Resurrection, nor purify them, and theirs will be a painful torment.

2.175 Those are they who have purchased error at the price of guidance, and torment at the price of forgiveness. So how bold they are (for evil deeds which will push them) to the Fire.

2.176 That is because Allah has sent down the Book (the Qur'an) in truth. And verily, those who disputed as regards the Book are far away in opposition.

The above Verses were revealed regarding the Jews (mainly their rabbis) who hid the description of Prophet Muhammad [PBUH] in their Books from the people. The reason why they did this was for worldly gain for they had high positions amongst the people and were always receiving gifts and money because they had the Tawrah and were regarded as religious. However, if the Jewish rabbis stated to the people that in their Books was the full description of the Prophet [PBUH] who would be sent to the whole of mankind, they would lose their status and worldly gains.

For this grave and evil sin, Allah will not speak to, nor purify, these Jews on the Day of Resurrection.

The second Verse above states that "they eat into their bellies nothing but fire" meaning whatever they gain for hiding the truth will turn into a raging fire in their stomachs on the Day of Resurrection. And where it says "so bold they are (for evil deeds which will push them) to the Fire" means that people will look at them on the Day of Resurrection, and they will be suffering and tormented to such an unimaginable degree that the people will be amazed at how they can bear the punishment.

The meaning of Al-Birr

2.177   **It is not Al-Birr (piety, righteousness) that you turn your faces towards east and (or) west (in prayers); but Al-Birr is the one who believes in Allah, the Last Day, the Angels, the Book, the Prophets and gives his wealth, in spite of love for it, to the kinsfolk, to the orphans, and to Al-Masakin (the poor), and to the wayfarer, and to those who ask, and to set servants free, performs As-Salat, and gives the Zakah, and who fulfill their covenant when they make it, and who are As-Sabirin (the patient) in extreme poverty and ailment (disease) and at the time of fighting (during the battles). Such are the people of the truth and they are Al-Muttaqun (the pious).**

The above Verse was revealed as follows: "The Jews used to face the west for their Qiblah, while the Christians used to face the east for their Qiblah. So Allah said: 'It is not Al-Birr that you turn your faces towards east and (or) west (in prayers)."'"cxxxix

Allah then states what is Al-Birr, including belief in Allah and Allah Alone, the Last Day, the angels and the Prophets; giving charity to the poor, beginning with relatives, followed by orphans, the poor, to strangers, and eventually those who ask for charity; to setting slaves free; performing the Salah, giving Zakah, fulfilling covenants, and who are patient when they are struck by a calamity or a disease.

Indeed, so vast is the meaning of the above Verse can be described as one which contains all aspects of Islam and righteousness.

Why is giving charity to relatives important? "Sadaqah (i.e. charity) given to the poor is a charity, while the Sadaqah given to the relatives is both Sadaqah and Silah (nurturing relations), for they are the most deserving of you and your kindness and charity."cxl

Who are the Masakin? Prophet Muhammad [PBUH] said: "The Miskin is not the person who roams around, and whose need is met by one or two dates or one or two bites. Rather, the Miskin is he who does not have what is sufficient, and to whom the people do not pay attention and, thus, do not give him from the charity."cxli

Al-Qisas – The Law of Equality

2.178 O you who believe! Al-Qisas (the Law of Equality in punishment) is prescribed for you in case of murder: the free for the free, the slave for the slave, and the female for the female. But if the killer is forgiven by the brother (or the relatives) of the killed (against blood money), then it should be sought in a good manner, and paid to him respectfully. This is an alleviation and a mercy from your Lord. So after this, whoever transgresses the limits (i.e. kills the killer after taking the blood money), he shall have a painful torment.

2.179 And there is (a saving of) life for you in Al-Qisas (the Law of Equality in punishment), O men of understanding, that you may acquire Taqwa.

The above Verses were revealed regarding the actions of two Jewish tribes before the arrival of Islam; one invaded the other and defeated them. They made it a law so that if the victorious tribe's man killed a defeated tribe's man, he is not killed in return but would have to pay a ransom. However, if the defeated tribe's man killed a victorious tribe's man, he is killed in return, or his family would have to pay double the ransom.

Hence, Allah Commanded the believers to be equitable in the law of punishment.

It is to be noted that where the above Verse states: "the free for the free, the slave for the slave, and the female for the female" – this was abrogated for "life for life" as is stated in Surah 5, Verse 45.

It is also stated that a Muslim should not be killed for a disbeliever whom he kills[cxlii].

But what if a group of people kill one person, should they all be punished? The Four Imams[cxliii] are agreed that the entire group should be killed and cite a story where seven men killed a boy in Yemen, 'Umar stated that if the whole of San'a had collaborated in carrying out the murder of the boy, then he would kill them all.

Allah also states in the above Verse that the family of the killed person can pardon the killer for intentional murder in return for blood money.

Allah also states "and there is (a saving of) life for you in Al-Qisas" – what this means is the killing the murderer has benefits as this preserves the sanctity of life because the killer will know that when he is caught, he will be killed.

The importance of the will

2.180   **It is prescribed for you, when death approaches any of you, if he leaves wealth, that he make a bequest to parents and next of kin, according to reasonable manners. (This is) a duty upon Al-Muttaqun (the pious).**

2.181   **Then whoever changes the bequest after hearing it, the sin shall be on those who make the change. Truly, Allah is All-Hearer, All-Knower.**

2.182   **But he who fears from a testator some unjust act or wrong-doing, and thereupon he makes peace between the parties concerned, there shall be no sin on him. Certainly, Allah is Oft-Forgiving, Most Merciful.**

The above Verse was revealed and was the law amongst the Muslims until it was abrogated when the Verse about inheritance was revealed.

The Prophet Muhammad [PBUH] commanded the Muslims to keep their will with them at all times:

"It is not permissible for any Muslim who has something to will to stay for two nights without having his last will and testament written and kept ready with him."[cxliv]

It is also important that the will is fair; Prophet Muhammad [PBUH] said:

"A man might perform the works of righteous people for seventy years, but when he dictates his will, he commits injustice and thus his works end with the worst of his deeds and he enters the Fire. A man might perform the works of evil people for seventy years, but then dictates a just will and thus ends with the best of his deeds and then enters Paradise."[cxlv]

Allah states: "then whoever changes the bequest after hearing it, the sin shall be on those who make the change" – this means that: "the dead person's reward will be preserved for him by Allah, while the sin is acquired by those who change the will."[cxlvi]

Allah states: "But he who fears from a testator some unjust act or wrong-doing" – this means that if there is an error or an unjust resolution so that some people get more and others less which is against the principles of the Islamic will, the executor of the will is permitted to correct these errors so that the Islamic law and the wishes of the dead person are respected.

The command to fast

2.183   **O you who believe! Fasting is prescribed for you as it was prescribed for those before you, that you may acquire Taqwa.**

2.184   **Fast for a fixed number of days, but if any of you is ill or on a journey, the same number (should be made up) from other days. And as for those who can fast with difficulty (e.g. an old man), they have (a choice either to fast or) to feed a Miskin (poor person) (for every day). But whoever does good of his own accord, it is better for him. And that you fast, it is better for you if only you know.**

Allah Commanded the Muslims to fast, meaning to abstain from food and drink and sexual activity for a fixed number of day, during set times during those days, and to do this purely for the sake of Allah.

The purpose of the fast is it to cleanse and purify the body from the evil of Shaytan.

Initially, "when the obligation to fast Ramadan was revealed, those who wished fasted, and those who wished did not (meaning they fed a poor person instead)."[cxlvii]

However, this was abrogated by Verse 2.185 and we shall come to that in the next Verse.

As for the elderly, it has been stated that: "it is for the old man and the old woman who are able to fast with difficulty, but choose instead to feed a poor person for every day (they do not fast)."[cxlviii]

With regard to a woman who is pregnant or breast-feeding, if she fears for herself or her children or her fetus, she can pay the Fidyah and she does not have to fast the days that she missed later on.

The month of Ramadan

2.185   **The month of Ramadan in which was revealed the Qur'an, a guidance for mankind and clear proofs for the guidance and the criterion (between right and wrong). So whoever of you sights (the crescent on the first night of) the month (of Ramadan i.e. is present at his home), he must observe Saum (fasting) that month, and whoever is ill or on a journey, the same number [of days which one did not observe Saum (fasting) must be made up] from other days. Allah intends for you ease, and He does not want to make things difficult for you. (He wants that you) must complete the same number (of days), and that you must magnify Allah [i.e. to say Takbir (Allahu-Akbar; Allah is the Most Great) on seeing the crescent of the months of Ramadan and Shawwal] for having guided you so that you may be grateful to Him.**

Allah states that the Qur'an was revealed during the month of Ramadan; in fact, all the Books were revealed during the month of Ramadan. Prophet Muhammad [PBUH] said:

> *"The Suhuf (pages) of Ibrahim were revealed during the first night of Ramadan. The Tawrah was revealed during the sixth night of Ramadan. The Injil was revealed during the thirteenth night of Ramadan. Allah revealed the Qur'an on the twenty-fourth night of Ramadan."*[cxlix]

Allah commands that if a person is healthy, sees the sighting of the moon while living in their own land, to commence the month of fasting (note, this Verse abrogated the previous Verse).

Next Allah states that if a person is ill, that person can forgo fasting and make up the missed number of days after the month of Ramadan.

As for those who are travelling, it is better not to fast; when asked about fasting whilst travelling, Prophet Muhammad [PBUH] said:

> *"Those who did not fast have done good, and there is no harm for those who fasted."*[cl]

If a person is fasting whilst travelling, but then finds the fast difficult, it is recommended that that person break the fast. When Prophet Muhammad [PBUH] saw a man who was being shaded by other people whilst travelling, he asked why he was being shaded; he was told that the man was fasting, to which he replied:

> *"It is not a part of Birr (piety) to fast while travelling."*[cli]

Regarding making up the missed days of fast, it is required that each person makes up each of the days but that these days do not have to be consecutive.

Allah responds to the invocations of His servants

2.186   **And when My servants ask you (O Muhammad [PBUH] concerning Me, then answer them), I am indeed near (to them by My Knowledge). I respond to the invocations of the supplicant when he calls on Me (without any mediator or intercessor). So let them obey in Me, so that they may be led aright.**

Allah will accept the supplication of His servants as long the servants ask Allah directly without a mediator or intercessor, and providing it meets two other criteria as the Prophet Muhammad [PBUH] said:

> *"No Muslim supplicates to Allah with a Du'a that does not involve sin or cutting the relations of the womb, but Allah will grant him one of the three things: He will either hasten the response to his supplication, save it for him until the Hereafter, or would turn an equivalent amount of evil away from him."*[clii]

Another hadith states:

> *"The supplication of the servant will be accepted as long as he does not supplicate for what includes sin, or cutting the relations of the womb, and as long as he does not become hasty. He was asked: 'O Messenger of Allah! How does one become hasty?' He said: 'He says, 'I supplicated and supplicated, but I do not see that my supplication is being accepted from me.' He thus loses interest and abandons supplicating (to Allah).'"*[cliii]

Prophet Muhammad [PBUH] also added that the supplication of three people will not be rejected:

> *"Three persons will not have their supplication rejected: the just ruler, the fasting person until breaking the fast, and the supplication of the oppressed person, for Allah raises it above the clouds on the Day of Resurrection, and the doors of heaven will be opened for it, and Allah says: 'By My grace! I will certainly grant it for you, even if after a while.'"*[cliv]

Eating, drinking and sexual relations are permitted during the night of Ramadan

> **2.187**　It is made lawful for you to have sexual relations with your wives on the night of As-Siyam (fasting). They are Libas [i.e. body cover, or screen], for you and you are Libas for them. Allah knows that you used to deceive yourselves, so He turned to you (accepted your repentance) and forgave you. So now have sexual relations with them and seek that which Allah has ordained for you (offspring), and eat and drink until the white thread (light) of dawn appears to you distinct from the black thread (darkness of night), then complete your fast till the nightfall. And do not have sexual relations with them (your wives) while you are in I'tikaf (i.e. confining oneself in a mosque for prayers and invocations) in the Masjids. These are the limits (set) by Allah, so approach them not. Thus does Allah make clear His Ayat (proofs, evidences, Verses lessons, signs etc.) to mankind that they may acquire Taqwa.

In the early years of Islam, the Muslims were not allowed to eat or drink or to have sexual relations after the 'Isha (Night) prayer (some said that the Muslims used to refrain from having sexual relations with their wives for the entire month of Ramadan[clv]); the Muslims found that difficult to do, hence Allah said: "Allah knows that you used to deceive yourselves, so He turned to you (accepted your repentance) and forgave you."

Hence, Allah permitted those fasting to eat and drink and have sexual relations with their wives until dawn.

As a result of this, if a person who is intending to begin the fast, if he has sexual relations with his wife, he will be in a state of Junub (meaning sexual impurity); however, it is permissible to begin the fast whilst in this state. In a hadith, a man asked the Prophet Muhammad [PBUH]:

> ""O Messenger of Allah! The (Dawn) prayer time starts while I am Junub, should I fast?" Allah's Messenger [PBUH] replied: "And I. The prayer time starts while I am Junub and I fast.""[clvi]

The Suhur meal is recommended

Eating the Suhur, the meal before the Fajr (morning) prayer for fasting is recommended and highly beneficial; Prophet Muhammad [PBUH] said:

> "Eat the Suhur, for there is blessing in Suhur."[clvii]

He also added:

> *"The distinction between our fast and the fast of the people of the Book is the meal of Suhur."*[clviii]

Another hadith states:

> *"Suhur is a blessed meal. Hence, do not abandon it, even if one just takes a sip of water. Indeed, Allah and His angels send Salah (blessings) upon those who eat Suhur."*[clix]

Prohibition of Al-Wisal (same title)

Continuing the fast throughout the night into the next day is not permitted; Prophet Muhammad [PBUH] stated:

> *"Do not practice al-Wisal in fasting. So, they (the Companions) said to him, "But you practice Al-Wisal, O Allah's Messenger!" The Prophet [PBUH] replied: "I am not like you, I am given food and drink during my sleep by my Lord."*[clx]

The food and drink that the Prophet [PBUH] was given was spiritual and not material.

Ruling on I'tikaf (same title)

Where the above Verse states I'tikaf, what is meant by this is: "This Verse is about the man who stays in I'tikaf at the mosque during Ramadan or other months, Allah prohibited him from touching (having sexual intercourse with) women, during the night or day, until he finishes his I'tikaf."[clxi]

Aside from sexual intercourse, the person is not allowed to kiss or embrace his wife when in I'tikaf; he is not even allowed to visit a sick person but may enquire about them.

The reason why I'tikaf is mentioned is that the Prophet Muhammad [PBUH] used to spend the last 10 nights of Ramadan in the Masjid.

The prohibition of bribery

2.188 **And eat up not one another's property unjustly (in any illegal way e.g. stealing, robbing, deceiving), nor give bribery to the rulers (judges before presenting your cases) that you may knowingly eat up a part of the property of others sinfully.**

The above Verse was revealed "about the indebted person when there is no evidence of the loan. So he denies taking the loan and the case goes to the authorities, even though he knows that it is not his money and that he is a sinner, consuming what is not allowed for him."[clxii]

Those who knowingly consume other people's property and those who deliberately mislead the judges who erroneously rule in their favor because of the false evidence, these people may win the case but on the Day of Judgment, they will have to answer Allah for their sins.

The above Verse has been transliterated further: "O son of Adam! Know that the judge's ruling does not allow you what is prohibited or prohibit you from what is allowed. The judge only rules according to his best judgment and according to the testimony of the witnesses. The judge is only human and is bound to make mistakes. Know that if the judge erroneously rules in someone's favor, then that person will still encounter the dispute when the disputing parties meet Allah on the Day of Resurrection."[clxiii]

The crescent moons

2.189 **They ask you (O Muhammad [PBUH]) about the crescents. Say: "These are signs to mark fixed periods of time for mankind and for the pilgrimage." It is not Al-Birr (piety, righteousness, etc.) that you enter the houses from the back but Al-Birr is from Taqwa. So enter houses through their proper doors, and have Taqwa of Allah that you may be successful.**

Prophet Muhammad [PBUH] described the crescents in detail:

"Allah has made the crescents signs to mark fixed periods of time for mankind. Hence, fast on seeing it (the crescent for Ramadan) and break the fast on seeing it (the crescent for Shawwal). If it (the crescent) was obscure to you then count thirty days (mark that month as thirty days)."[clxiv]

Regarding entering the houses: "When some people during the time of Jahiliyyah would leave home to travel, and then decide not to travel, they would not enter the house from its door. Rather, they would climb over the back wall; Allah then revealed: 'It is not Al-Birr (piety, righteousness) that you enter the houses from the back.'"[clxv]

The first Verse revealed about Jihad

2.190   And fight in the Way of Allah those who fight you, but transgress not the limits. Truly, Allah likes not the transgressors.

2.191   And kill them wherever you find them, and turn them out from where they have turned you out. And Al-Fitnah is worse than killing. And fight not with them at Al-Masjid-al-Haram (the sanctuary at Makkah), unless they (first) fight you there. But if they attack you, then kill them. Such is the recompense of the disbelievers.

2.192   But if they cease, then Allah is Oft-Forgiving, Most Merciful.

2.193   And fight them until there is no more Fitnah (disbelief and worshipping of others along with Allah) and (all and every kind of) worship is for Allah (Alone). But if they cease, let there be no transgression except against Az-Zalimin (the polytheists and wrong-doers).

"This was the first Verse about fighting that was revealed in Al-Madinah. Ever since it was revealed, Allah's Messenger [PBUH] used to fight only those who fought him and avoid non-combatants. Later, Surah 9 was revealed."[clxvi] The Verse in Surah 9 [9.36] supplemented the above Verse.

Where the above Verse states 'turn them out', this means that you should spend your energy and resources in fighting the disbelievers, just as the disbelievers use their energy and resources to fight you, and you should expel them from the lands that they have expelled you. This was in reference to the law of Al-Qisas, the equality in punishment.

However, the above Verse also states: 'but transgress not the limits.' What this means is that you should not retaliate in a vengeful manner with acts that the disbelievers committed against you if it is against the law of Allah. Prophet Muhammad [PBUH] stated:

> *"Fight for the sake of Allah and fight those who disbelieve in Allah. Fight, but do not steal (from the captured goods), commit treachery, mutilate (the dead), or kill a child, or those who reside in houses of worship."*[clxvii]

It is also stated: "A woman was found dead during one of the Prophet's battles and the Prophet [PBUH] then forbade killing women and children."[clxviii]

Shirk is worse than killing (same title)

Allah states: "And Al-Fitnah is worse than killing." This means that those who commit Shirk (polytheists) are committing a worse act than those who kill.

Fighting in Al-Masjid Al-Haram

Allah states that fighting in the sacred area of Al-Masjid Al-Haram is strictly prohibited; however, if someone does start fighting in it, you are commanded to fight them and to kill them to stop their aggression.

There was one occasion when fighting was permitted in Al-Masjid Al-Haram and that was when Prophet Muhammad [PBUH] and the Muslims conquered the city; he said: "fighting in it was made legal for me only for an hour in the daytime . . . If anyone mentions the fighting in it that occurred by Allah's Messenger, then say that Allah allowed His Messenger, but did not allow you."[clxix]

The Command to fight until there is no more Fitnah (same title)

Allah states: "And fight them until there is no more Fitnah." This means that you should fight them until the religion of Allah becomes dominant above all other religions.

The prohibition of fighting in the sacred months

2.194 **The sacred month is for the sacred month, and for the prohibited things, there is the Law of Equality (Qisas). Then whoever transgresses against you, you transgress likewise against him. And fear Allah, and know that Allah is with Al-Muttaqin.**

This is best described as follows: "Allah's Messenger [PBUH] would not engage in warfare during the Sacred Month unless he was first attacked, then he would march forth. He would otherwise remain idle until the end of the Sacred Months."[clxx]

The Command to spend in the cause of Allah

2.195   **And spend in the cause of Allah (i.e. Jihad of all kinds) and do not throw yourselves into destruction (by not spending your wealth in the cause of Allah), and do good. Truly, Allah loves Al-Muhsinun (the good-doers).**

Allah Commands you to spend in His cause, meaning to spend on fighting and on what strengthens the Muslims against the disbelievers. And Allah warns that those who do not spend in Allah's cause and who refrain from aiding the Muslims against the enemy will face 'destruction'.

The Ruling on those who cannot complete the Hajj and 'Umrah

2.196 And complete Hajj and 'Umrah (i.e. the pilgrimage to Makkah) for Allah. But if you are prevented (from completing them), then sacrifice a Hady (an animal, i.e. a sheep, a cow, or a camel) such as you can afford, and do not shave your heads until the Hady reaches the place of sacrifice. And whosoever of you is ill or has an ailment in his scalp (necessitating shaving), he must pay a Fidyah (ransom) of either fasting or giving Sadaqah (charity) or offering a sacrifice. Then if you are in safety and whosoever performs the 'Umrah (in the months of Hajj), before (performing) the Hajj, he must slaughter a Hady such as he can afford, but if he cannot (afford it), he should fast for three days during the Hajj and seven days after his return (to his home), making ten days in all. This is for him whose family is not present at Al-Masjid-al-Haram (i.e. non-resident of Makkah). And fear Allah much and know that Allah is severe in punishment.

The above Verse was revealed in the 6th year of Hijrah, when the polytheists of the Quraysh prevented the Prophet [PBUH] and the Muslims from performing the pilgrimage to Makkah.

Allah begins the Verse by stating that if a person commences Hajj and 'Umrah, that person must complete them. It also means: "complete Hajj and 'Umrah, performing each of them separately, and to perform 'Umrah outside of the months of Hajj, for Allah the Exalted says: 'The Hajj (pilgrimage) is (in) the well-known (lunar year) months [Verse 2.197].'"[clxxi]

However, if a person is prevented from completing the pilgrimage, that person should slaughter an animal (Hady), shave the head and end Ihram. "The Hady includes eight types of animals: camels, cows, goats and sheep."[clxxii] However, the person should not shave their heads until the Hady reached the place of sacrifice. Then, the person ends the rituals of Hajj or 'Umrah.

Regarding what can prevent a person from completing the pilgrimage, it includes someone becoming ill and getting lost on the way; Prophet Muhammad [PBUH] also added: "Whoever suffered a broken bone or a limb, will have ended his Ihram and has to perform Hajj again."[clxxiii]

Allah then states that whoever shaved his head during Ihram will have to pay the Fidyah. The ruling on this has been described by one of the Companions by the name of Ka'b: "This was revealed concerning my case especially, but it is also for you in general. I was carried to Allah's Messenger [PBUH] and the lice were falling in great numbers on my face. The Prophet [PBUH] said: 'I never thought that your ailment (or struggle) had reached to such an extent as I can see. Can you afford a sheep (for sacrifice)?' I replied in the negative. He then said: 'Fast for three days or feed six poor persons, each with half a Sa' of food (with 1 Sa' equal to 3 kg) and shave your head.'"[clxxiv]

In the above hadith, the Prophet Muhammad [PBUH] offered the Companion what earned the highest reward: sacrificing an animal is the highest reward, followed by feeding six poor persons, then followed by fasting for three days.

Allah then states that if a person performs the 'Umrah in the months of Hajj before performing the Hajj (known as Tamattu'), then that person must slaughter a Hady if he is able, and if not that person must fast for three days during the Hajj followed by fasting for seven further days when he returns back to his home, thus resulting in ten days of fasting in total. As for which days the person should fast, these are "one day before the day of Tarwiyah, the day of Tarwiyah (8th day of Dhul-Hijjah) and then 'Arafah day (9th day of Dhul-Hijjah)."[clxxv] However, if one is not able to fast these three days or some of them before Eid day (10th of Dhul-Hijjah), he is then allowed to fast during the Tashriq days (11th to 13th of Dhul-Hijjah).

Allah states that those are residents of Makkah, they do not perform Tamattu'.

The Rulings on Hajj

2.197 **The Hajj (pilgrimage) is (in) the well-known (lunar year) months. So whosoever intends to perform Hajj therein (by assuming Ihram), then he should not have sexual relations (with his wife), nor commit sin, nor dispute unjustly during the Hajj. And whatever good you do, Allah knows it. And take provisions for the journey, but the best provision is At-Taqwa (piety, righteousness). So fear Me, O men of understanding!**

When is Hajj? This is in the "Shawwal (10th month of Islamic Calendar), Dhul-Qa'dah (11th month) and the (first) ten days of Dhul-Hijjah (12th month)."[clxxvi]

As for assuming Ihram, "this occurs during the months of Hajj."[clxxvii] This means that "no person should assume Ihram for Hajj before the months of Hajj."[clxxviii]

The conditions following assuming Ihram are that the person should not have sexual relations with his wife (including anything that leads to this, including embracing, kissing or talking about such things[clxxix]), nor committing sins (meaning all acts of disobedience of Allah), nor arguing unjustly during the Hajj.

The Prophet Muhammad [PBUH] stated:

> *"Whoever performed Hajj to this (Sacred) House and did not commit Rafath (sexual intercourse) or Fusuq (commit sins), will return sinless, just as the day his mother gave birth to him."[clxxx]*

Allah also Commands people to perform righteous good deeds and informs the believers that He is aware of each and every deed.

Regarding the provisions, this was related to the people of Yemen who would set out for the Hajj without any provision, and said that they were people who had Tawakkul (reliance on Allah). However, Allah forbade this practice and commanded all those who go for the pilgrimage to take sufficient provisions for them. However, Allah also stated to the pilgrims that whilst they must take sustenance with them for the journey, the best provision for each pilgrim is to be pious and righteous (to have Taqwa).

Commercial Transactions During Hajj

2.198   **There is no sin on you if you seek the Bounty of your Lord (during pilgrimage by trading). Then when you leave 'Arafat, remember Allah (by glorifying His Praises, i.e. prayers and invocations) at the Mash'ar-il-Haram. And remember Him (by invoking Allah for all good) as He has guided you, and verily you were before, of those who were astray.**

Allah states that a person who is performing the Hajj can carry out business transaction and trade in goods.

Standing at 'Arafat

When does a pilgrim stand on 'Arafat? This starts from noon on the day of 'Arafah (9th day of Dhul-Hijjah, the 12th month) until dawn the next day, the day of the Sacrifice (10th day of Dhul-Hijjah).

Prophet Muhammad [PBUH] stated:

> *"Hajj is 'Arafat (thrice). Hence, those who have stood at 'Arafat before dawn will have performed (the rituals of the Hajj). The days of Mina are three, and there is no sin for those who move on after two days, or for those who stay."*[clxxxi]

What is Al-Mash'ar Al-Haram? It has been described as all of Al-Muzdalifah[clxxxii] and the Mount and the surrounding area[clxxxiii].

2.199   **Then depart from the place whence all the people depart and ask Allah for His forgiveness. Truly, Allah is Oft-Forgiving, Most-Merciful.**

The above Verse was revealed because the "Quraysh and their allies, who used to be called Al-Hums[clxxxiv], used to stay in Al-Muzdalifah while the rest of the Arabs would stand at 'Arafat. When Islam came, Allah commanded His Prophet [PBUH] to stand at 'Arafat and then proceed from there."[clxxxv]

And Allah Commands His servants to seek His forgiveness (this is repeated throughout the Qur'an). Prophet Muhammad [PBUH] used to seek forgiveness after each Salah (prayer) by saying Tasbih (saying "Subhan Allah", meaning Glorified is Allah) 33 times, Tahmid (saying "Al-Hamdu Lillah", meaning praise be to Allah) 33 times, and Takbir (saying "Allahu Akbar", meaning Allah is the Most Great) 33 times.[clxxxvi]

Prophet Muhammad also stated:

> *"The master of supplication for forgiveness, is for the servant to say:*

"O Allah! You are my Lord, there is no deity worthy of worship except You. You have created me and I am Your servant. I am on Your covenant, as much as I can be, and awaiting Your promise. I seek refuge with You from the evil that I have committed. I admit Your favor on me and admit my faults. So forgive me, for none except You forgives the sins."

"Whoever said these words at night and died that same night will enter Paradise. Whoever said it during the day and died will enter Paradise."[clxxxvii]

The Command to Remember Allah After Hajj and Seek His Aid Both in This Life and The Hereafter

2.200 So when you have accomplished your Manasik, remember Allah as you remember your forefathers or with far more remembrance. But of mankind there are some who say: "Our Lord! Give us (Your bounties) in this world!" and for such there will be no portion in the Hereafter.

2.201 And of them there are some who say: "Our Lord! Give us in this world that which is good and in the Hereafter that which is good, and save us from the torment of the Fire!"

2.202 For them there will be allotted a share for what they have earned. And Allah is Swift at reckoning.

The first part of the above Verse was revealed as follows: "During the time of Jahiliyyah, people used to stand during the (Hajj) season, and one of them would say: 'My father used to feed (the poor), help others, pay the Diyah (blood money),' and so forth. The only Dhikr that they had was that they would remember the deeds of their fathers. Allah then revealed to Muhammad [PBUH]: 'Remember Allah as you remember your forefathers or with far more remembrance'."clxxxviii

Allah also criticized those who only supplicate for the good of this world without any regard for the Hereafter. However, He praised those who ask for both the good of this world and in the Hereafter.

The Ruling on The Tashriq Days

2.203 **And remember Allah during the Appointed Days. But whosoever hastens to leave in two days, there is no sin on him and whosoever stays on, there is no sin on him, if his aim is to do good and obey Allah (fear Him), and know that you will surely be gathered unto Him.**

"The Appointed Days are the Days of Tashriq (11th to 13th of Dhul-Hijjah)."[clxxxix]

Prophet Muhammad [PBUH] added:

"The day of 'Arafah (9th of Dhul-Hijjah), the day of the Sacrifice (10th) and the days of the Tashriq (11th to 13th) are our Eid (festival) for we people of Islam. These are days of eating and drinking."[cxc]

Allah Commands us to recite the Takbir (saying "Allahu Akbar" – meaning Allah is the Most Great) during the days of Tashriq after the compulsory prayers.[cxci]

Prophet Muhammad [PBUH] also stated:

"Do not fast these days (i.e. Tashriq Days), for they are days of eating, drinking and remembering Allah the Exalted and Most Honored."[cxcii]

Regarding the Verse "But whosoever hastens to leave in two days . . .", what it hints to is the three days after the Day of Sacrifice.

Characteristics of The Hypocrites

2.204   **And of mankind there is he whose speech may please you (O Muhammad [PBUH]), in this worldly life, and he calls Allah to witness as to that which is in his heart, yet he is the most quarrelsome of the opponents.**

2.205   **And when he turns away (from you O Muhammad [PBUH]), his effort in the land is to make mischief therein and to destroy the crops and the cattle, and Allah likes not mischief.**

2.206   **And when it is said to him: "Fear Allah", he is led by arrogance to (more) crime. So enough for him is Hell, and worst indeed is that place to rest!**

2.207   **And of mankind is he who would sell himself, seeking the pleasure of Allah. And Allah is full of Kindness to (His) servants.**

Prophet Muhammad [PBUH] said:

> *"The signs of a hypocrite are three: Whenever he speaks, he tells a lie. Whenever he promises, he always breaks it (his promise). If you have a dispute with him, he is most quarrelsome."*[cxciii]

He also added:

> *"The most hated person to Allah is he who is Aladd and Khasim (meaning most quarrelsome)."*[cxciv]

The hypocrites are particularly deviant and we should be aware of them: "they (hypocrites) are people who use the religion to gain material benefit. Their tongues are sweeter than honey, but their hearts are more bitter than Sabir (a bitter plant, aloe). They show the people the appearance of sheep while their hearts hide the viciousness of wolves. Allah said: 'They dare challenge Me, but they are deceived by Me. I swear by Myself that I will send a Fitnah (trial, calamity) on them that will make the wise man bewildered.'"[cxcv]

The Command to Enter Islam in its Entirety

2.208   O you who believe! Enter Silm (Islam) perfectly, and follow not the footsteps of Shaytan (Satan). Verily, he is to you a plain enemy.

2.209   Then if you slide back after the clear signs (Prophet Muhammad [PBUH], and this Qur'an, and Islam) have come to you, then know that Allah is All-Mighty, All-Wise.

The above Verses were revealed about a group of the People of the Scripture who became believers but still followed parts of the Tawrah. Hence, Allah Commanded them in particular and mankind in general to follow all aspects of Islam.

And Allah warns that if you do not follow Islam after all signs have become apparent (meaning Prophet Muhammad [PBUH], the Qur'an and Islam), then His punishment will be severe.

2.210   Do they then wait for anything other than that Allah should come to them over the shadows of the clouds and the angels? (Then) the case would be already judged. And to Allah return all matters (for decision).

The Punishment for Changing Allah's Favor and Mocking the Believers

2.211 Ask the Children of Israel how many clear Ayat (proofs, evidences, verses, lessons, signs, revelations, etc.) We gave them. And whoever changes Allah's favor after it has come to him, [e.g. renounces the Religion of Allah (Islam) and accepts Kufr (disbelief)] then surely, Allah is severe in punishment.

2.212 Beautified is the life of this world for those who disbelieve, and they mock at those who believe. But those who have Taqwa, will be above them on the Day of Resurrection. And Allah gives (of His bounty, blessings, favors and honors on the Day of Resurrection) to whom He wills without limit.

The above Verses begin by mentioning the miracles and signs that the Children of Israel witnessed during the time of Musa, and yet they disbelieved time and time again. Allah then warns those who become believers in Allah and the religion of Islam but who then turn to disbelief; they will face a severe punishment. These disbelievers love the life of this world and mock those who are true believers; their life revolves around hoarding wealth that Allah has bestowed upon them but refrain from spending in the cause of Allah. Regarding this, Prophet Muhammad [PBUH] said:

"Every day two angels come down from heavens and one of them says: 'O Allah! Compensate every person who spends in Your cause,' and the other (angel) says: 'O Allah! Destroy every miser.'"[cxcvi]

Allah Sent The Prophets After Mankind Disputed

2.213 **Mankind were one community and Allah sent Prophets with glad tidings and warnings, and with them He sent the Scripture in truth to judge between people in matters wherein they differed. And only those to whom (the Scripture) was given differed concerning it, after clear proofs had come unto them, through hatred, one to another. Then Allah by His leave guided those who believed to the truth of that wherein they differed. And Allah guides whom He wills to the straight path.**

The above Verse has been described as follows: "There were ten generations between Adam and Nuh, all of them on the religion of Truth. They later disputed so Allah sent the Prophets as warners and bringers of glad tidings."[cxcvii] Hence, the first Prophet to be sent to the people was Nuh.[cxcviii]

Allah then states that those who received the Scripture differed through hatred of one another. There is a detailed description about this: "They disputed about the day of Congregation (Friday). The Jews made it Saturday while the Christians chose Sunday. Allah guided the Ummah of Muhammad [PBUH] to Friday. They also disputed about the true Qiblah. The Christians faced the east while the Jews faced Bayt Al-Maqdis. Allah guided the Ummah of Muhammad [PBUH] to the true Qiblah (Kaabah in Makkah). They also disputed about the prayer, as some of them bow down, but do not prostrate, while others prostrate, but do not bow down. Some of them pray while talking and some while walking. Allah guided the Ummah of Muhammad [PBUH] to the truth. They also disputed about the fast; some of them fast during a part of the day, while others fast from certain types of foods. Allah guided the Ummah of Muhammad [PBUH] to the truth. They also disputed about Ibrahim. The Jews said: 'He was a Jew,' while the Christians considered him Christian. Allah has made him a Haniyfan Musliman. Allah has guided the Ummah of Muhammad [PBUH] to the truth. They also disputed about 'Isa. The Jews rejected him and accused his mother of a grave sin, while the Christians made him a god and the son of God. Allah made him by His Word and a spirit from Him. Allah guided the Ummah of Muhammad [PBUH] to the truth."[cxcix]

Prophet Muhammad [PBUH] also added:

"We are the last (nation), but the first (foremost) on the Day of Resurrection. We are the first people to enter Paradise, although they (Jews and Christians) have been given the Book before us and we after them. Allah has guided us to the truth wherever they disputed over it. This is the day (Friday) that they disputed about, Allah guided us to it. So, the people follow us, as tomorrow is for the Jews and the day after is for the Christians."[cc]

Victory Only Comes After Succeeding in Allah's Trials

2.214 **Or think you that you will enter Paradise without such (trials) as came to those who passed away before you? They were afflicted with severe poverty and ailments and were so shaken that even the Messenger and those who believed along with him said: "When (will come) the help of Allah?" Yes! Certainly, the help of Allah is near!**

Allah states that you will be tested and tried with various trials that previous nations were afflicted with. During the time of Prophet Muhammad [PBUH], one of the Companions stated: "We said: 'O Messenger of Allah! Why did you not invoke Allah to support us? Why do you not supplicate to Allah for us? He said:

"The saw would be placed on the middle of the head of one of those who were before you (believers) and he would be sawn until his feet, and he would be combed with iron combs between his skin and bones, yet that would not make him change his religion.""[cci]

And Allah states that succeeding in these trials, remaining steadfast and placing your trust in Allah, and living according to the Qur'an and the Sunnah of Prophet Muhammad [PBUH] during times of distress will result in Paradise in the Hereafter.

The Rulings on Spending Charity

2.215   **They ask you (O Muhammad [PBUH]) what they should spend. Say: "Whatever you spend of good must be for parents and kindred and orphans and Al-Masakin (the poor) and the wayfarers, and whatever you do of good deeds, truly, Allah knows it well.**

The above Verse is about the voluntary charity[ccii]. The ones who deserve charity the most are: "your mother, father, sister, brother, the closest and then the farthest (relatives)."[cciii]

Jihad is Made Obligatory

2.216 **Fighting is ordained for you (Muslims) though you dislike it, and it may be that you dislike a thing which is good for you and that you like a thing which is bad for you. Allah knows but you do not know.**

In the above Verse Allah made Jihad obligatory on the Muslims. It is stated that: "Jihad is required from every person, whether he actually joins the fighting or remains behind. Whoever remains behind is required to give support, if support is warranted; to provide aid, if aid is needed; and to march forth, if he is commanded to do so. If he is not needed, then he remains behind."[cciv]

It is also stated:

> "Whoever dies but neither fought (i.e. in Allah's cause), nor sincerely considered fighting, will die a death of Jahiliyyah (pre-Islamic era of ignorance)."[ccv]

Ruling on Fighting During the Sacred Months

2.217   **They ask you concerning fighting in the Sacred Months (i.e. 1st, 7th, 11th and 12th months of the Islamic calendar). Say: "Fighting therein is a great (transgression) but a greater (transgression) with Allah is to prevent mankind from following the way of Allah, to disbelieve in Him, to prevent access to Al-Masjid-al-Haram (at Makkah), and to drive out its inhabitants, and Al-Fitnah is worse than killing." And they will never cease fighting you until they turn you back from your religion (Islamic Monotheism) if they can. And whosoever of you turns back from his religion and dies as a disbeliever, then his deeds will be lost in this life and in the Hereafter, and they will be the dwellers of the Fire. They will abide therein forever.**

2.218   **Verily, those who have believed, and those who have emigrated (for Allah's religion) and have striven hard in the way of Allah, all these hope for Allah's Mercy. And Allah is Oft-Forgiving, Most-Merciful.**

The above Verses were revealed following the Nakhlah Military Manoeuvres: After the Battle of Badr, during the month of Rajab, Prophet Muhammad [PBUH] sent 'Abdullah bin Jahsh on an expedition with eight other men; he gave 'Abdullah a letter and told him not to open it until they had marched for two days. When they had marched for two days, 'Abdullah opened the letter: "When you read these instructions, march until you set camp at Nakhlah between Makkah and At-Ta'if. There, watch the movements of the caravan of Quraysh and collect news about them for us." A caravan which belonged to the Quraysh passed by carrying various goods. The Companions discussed the situation amongst themselves, which was the last day in the sacred month of Rajab. The options were that either they let them pass, but when they entered the Sacred Area they would be safe from them; or, they could kill them, but they were still in the sacred month of Rajab. One of the Companions shot an arrow and killed one of those in the caravan, whist the others either gave themselves up or fled the scene. When they returned back to the Prophet [PBUH], he said to them: "I have not commanded you to conduct warfare during the Sacred Month." The Prophet [PBUH] did left them and did not take any of the war booty. The other Companions began to criticize those who went on the expedition and killed one of the disbelievers. However, then Allah revealed the above Verse.

Allah states that Fitnah is a greater transgression than killing.

Allah then explains that the disbelievers will never rest until you give up the religion of Islam, and if you do, you will end up in the Fire just as the other disbelievers. But those who have faith in Allah, who emigrate for His cause, and who strive hard in the way of Allah, they have hope that the Almighty will forgive them and reward them in the Hereafter.

The Gradual Prohibition of Khamr (alcoholic drink)

2.219 **They ask you (O Muhammad [PBUH]) concerning alcoholic drink and gambling. Say: "In them is a great sin, and (some) benefits for men, but the sin of them is greater than their benefit." And they ask you what they ought to spend. Say: "That which is (spare) beyond your needs." Thus Allah makes clear to you His Laws in order that you may give thought.**

2.220 **In (to) this worldly life and in the Hereafter. And they ask you concerning orphans. Say: "The best thing is to work honestly in their property, and if you mix your affairs with theirs, then they are your brothers. And Allah knows (the one) who means mischief (e.g. to swallow their property) from (the one) who means good (e.g. to save their property). And if Allah had wished, He could have put you into difficulties. Truly, Allah is All-Mighty, All-Wise."**

The above Verse was the first (of three Verses) to be revealed about the prohibition of consuming alcohol. It has been stated that 'Umar once said: "O Allah! Give us a clear ruling regarding Al-Khmar!" Allah revealed the above Verse. When 'Umar read the Verse he said again: "O Allah! Give us a clear ruling regarding Al-Khamr." Allah then revealed in Verse 4.43: "O you who believe! Approach not As-Salah (the prayer) when you are in a drunken state." However, 'Umar said for a third time: "O Allah! Give us a clear ruling regarding Al-Khamr." Then Allah revealed in Verse 5.91: "So, will you not then abstain." 'Umar then said: "We did abstain, we did abstain."[ccvi]

'Umar added: "it includes all what intoxicates the mind."

Spending money on charity

Prophet Muhammad [PBUH] said:

> "Start with yourself and grant it some charity. If anything remains, then spend it on your family. If anything remains, then spend it on your relatives. If anything remains, then spend it like this and like that (i.e. on various charitable purposes)."[ccvii]

Maintaining the orphan's property

Before the above Verse was revealed, the people looking after orphans would keep their food and drink separate from their own, until the orphans would take it or until it got spoilt. This was difficult for them, hence Allah revealed the above Verse. Allah permitted the executor of the orphan's estate to spend from it, as long as it is in reasonable amounts, as long as he has the intention to compensate the orphan later on. (see Surah Nisa)

Prohibition of Marrying Mushrik Men and Women

2.221 **And do not marry Al-Mushrikat (idolatresses) till they believe (worship Allah Alone). And indeed a slave woman who believes is better than a (free) Mushrikah (idolatress), even though she pleases you. And give not (your daughters) in marriage to Al-Mushrikin till they believe (in Allah Alone) and verily, a believing servant is better than a (free) Mushrik (idolater), even though he pleases you. Those (Mushrikin) invite you to the Fire, but Allah invites (you) to Paradise and forgiveness by His leave, and makes His Ayat (proofs, evidences, verses, lessons, signs, revelations, etc.) clear to mankind that they may remember.**

Allah has prohibited the believers from marrying Mushrik men or women (the idolaters and idolatresses) and has stated that it is better to marry a believing servant than a rich and powerful idolater or idolatress. And where it says: "those (Mushrikin) invite you to the Fire", this means that mixing, associating and befriending the disbelievers will ultimately indulge one to love the life of this life over the Hereafter, and therefore lead one to the Fire, may Allah save us from this.

One of the Companions said: "Allah has excluded the women of the People of the Scripture."[ccviii] Ibn 'Umar, however, had his own interpretation of this and said: "I do not know of a bigger Shirk than her saying that Jesus is her Lord!"[ccix]

Prophet Muhammad [PBUH] said:

> *"The life of this world is but a delight, and the best of the delights of this earthly life is the righteous wife."*[ccx]

He also said:

> *"A woman is chosen for marriage for four reasons: her wealth, social status, beauty and religion. So, marry the religious woman, may your hands be filled with sand (a statement of encouragement)."*[ccxi]

Prohibition of Sexual Intercourse With Menstruating Women

2.222   **They ask you concerning menstruation. Say: "That is an Adha (a harmful thing for a husband to have a sexual intercourse with his wife while she is having her menses), therefore, keep away from women during menses and go not unto them till they are purified (from menses and have taken a bath)." And when they have purified themselves, then go in unto them as Allah has ordained for you. Truly, Allah loves those who turn unto Him in repentance and loves those who purify themselves (by taking a bath and cleaning and washing thoroughly their private parts, bodies, for their prayers, etc.).**

2.223   **Your wives are a tilth for you, so go to your tilth (have sexual relations with your wives in any manner as long as it is in the vagina and not in the anus), when or how you will, and send (good deeds, or ask Allah to bestow upon you pious offspring) before you for your ownselves. And fear Allah, and know that you are to meet Him (in the Hereafter), and give good tidings to the believers (O Muhammad).**

The above Verses were revealed after the Companions asked the Prophet Muhammad [PBUH] about the practice of the Jews, who would not have sexual intercourse with their women who were menstruating; in fact, they would not eat or even mix with them in the house when they were menstruating. Then, Allah revealed the above Verses.

The Prophet [PBUH] explained the above Verse as: **"Do anything you wish except having sexual intercourse."**[ccxii] A hadith adds: "Whenever the Prophet [PBUH] wanted to fondle any of his wives during the periods (menses), he used to ask her to wear an Izar (a sheet covering the lower-half of the body)."[ccxiii]

Once her menstruation is over, men are then permitted to have sexual intercourse with them as long as they have purified themselves (by taking a bath) or they have performed Tayammum with sand if water is not available.

Where the above Verse states: "Your wives are a tilth for you," this means "the place of pregnancy."[ccxiv] Prophet Muhammad [PBUH] said:

> *"If anyone of you on having sexual relations with his wife said: 'In the Name of Allah. O Allah! Protect us from Shaytan and also protect what you bestow upon us (i.e. the coming offspring) from Shaytan,' and if it is destined that they should have a child then, Shaytan will never be able to harm him."*[ccxv]

And as the above Verse states, anal sex is forbidden. Prophet Muhammad [PBUH] said:

> *"Allah does not look at a man who had anal sex with another man or a woman."*[ccxvi]

Some scholars have even stated that anyone who performs anal sex is a Kufr.

Prohibition of Swearing to Abandon a Good Deed

2.224   And make not Allah's (Name) an excuse in your oaths against doing good and acting piously, and making peace among mankind. And Allah is All-Hearer, All-Knower (i.e. do not swear much and if you have sworn against doing something good then give an expiation for the oath and do good).

2.225   Allah will not call you to account for that which is unintentional in your oaths, but He will call you to account for that which your hearts have earned. And Allah is Oft-Forgiving, Most-Forbearing.

The above Verse is explained as: "Do not vow to refrain from doing good works. (If you make such vow then) break it, pay the Kaffarah (meaning expiation) and do the good work."[ccxvii] In the situation where one swears an oath but then finds a better deed, Prophet Muhammad [PBUH] said:

> *"Whoever makes a vow and then finds what is better than his vow (should break his vow), pay the Kaffarah and perform the better deed."*[ccxviii]

As for the unintentional vows (known in Arabic as Laghw vows), Allah will not hold you to account. What are the unintentional vows? Prophet Muhammad [PBUH] said:

> *"The Laghw in the vows includes what the man says in his house, such as, 'No, by Allah,' and 'Yes, by Allah.'"*[ccxix]

They also "include vowing while angry."[ccxx]

The Rulings on Ila'

2.226 **Those who take an oath not to have sexual relation with their wives must wait four months, then if they return, verily, Allah is Oft-Forgiving, Most Merciful.**

2.227 **And if they decide upon divorce, then Allah is All-Hearer, All-Knower.**

The Ila' is a vow that a man makes not to have sexual relations with his wife for a certain period of time. If it is for a period less than four months, the man has to wait for the end of the vow period before he can then have sexual relations with his wife; in this scenario, the wife cannot ask her husband to have sexual relations with her. However, if the vow is longer than four months, the wife is allowed to ask her husband to end the Ila' and have sexual relations with her at the end of the four months. Otherwise, the husband should divorce his wife after the four month period; however, if he refuses to divorce her, the authorities have the right to force the divorce in order to protect the wife. On a final point on this, the divorce does not automatically occur at the end of the four month period; either the man returns to his wife or he should divorce her or be forced to divorce her.[ccxxi]

Rulings on the 'Iddah (waiting period) of the Divorced Woman

2.228 **And divorced women shall wait (as regards their marriage) for three menstrual periods, and it is not lawful for them to conceal what Allah has created in their wombs, if they believe in Allah and the Last Day. And their husbands have the better right to take them back in that period, if they wish for reconciliation. And they (women) have rights (over their husbands as regards living expenses) similar (to those of their husbands) over them (as regards obedience and respect) to what is reasonable, but men have a degree (of responsibility) over them. And Allah is All-Mighty, All-Wise.**

The above Verse states that the divorced woman has to wait for three menstrual periods (if she still has menstruation periods) after the divorce before she can remarry if she chooses. Until this period ends, she is still the wife of her husband[ccxxii].

During the period between when the husband says divorce and the three menstruation periods, the woman may be pregnant; Allah has stated that only the woman will know if she is pregnant, and if she is she must disclose this to the husband.

And the husband has the right to then take her back if he so chooses (but the husband can only take his wife back twice, and on the third divorce it becomes final – see next Verse).

What rights does a wife have? Prophet Muhammad [PBUH] stated:

"Fear Allah regarding your women, for you have taken them by Allah's covenant and were allowed to enjoy with them sexually by Allah's Words. You have the right on them that they do not allow anyone you dislike to sit on your mat. If they do that, then discipline then leniently. They have the right to be spent on and to be bought clothes in what is reasonable."[ccxxiii]

In addition, one of the Companions asked: "O Messenger of Allah! What is the right the wife of one of us has?" The Prophet [PBUH] said:

"To feed her when you eat, buy her clothes when you buy for yourself and to refrain from striking her on the face, cursing her or staying away from her except in the house."[ccxxiv]

Rulings on Divorce

2.229   The divorce is twice, after that either you retain her on reasonable terms or release her with kindness. And it is not lawful for you (men) to take back (from your wives) any of your Mahr (bridal money given by the husband to his wife at the time of marriage) which you have given them, except when both parties fear that they would be unable to keep the limits ordained by Allah (e.g. to deal with each other on a fair basis). Then if you fear that they would not be able to keep the limits ordained by Allah, then there is no sin on either of them if she gives back (the Mahr or a part of it). These are the limits ordained by Allah, so do not transgress them. And whoever transgresses the limits ordained by Allah, then such are the Zalimun (wrong-doers).

2.230   And if he has divorced her (the third time), then she is not lawful unto him thereafter until she has married another husband. Then, if the other husband divorces her, it is no sin on both of them that they reunite, provided they feel that they can keep the limits ordained by Allah. These are the limits of Allah, which He makes plain for the people who have knowledge.

As Allah states in the above Verse, divorce is thrice: "When the man divorces his wife twice, let him fear Allah, regarding the third time. He should either keep her with him and treat her with kindness, or let her go her own way with kindness, without infringing upon any of her rights."[ccxxv]

It is also stated that pronouncing divorce three times at same time is unlawful. When the Prophet Muhammad [PBUH] heard about a man who said divorce three times in succession, the Prophet [PBUH] got up angry and said:

> *"The Book of Allah is being made the subject of jest while I am still amongst you."*[ccxxvi]

Why was three divorces legislated in the Qur'an? Before this Verse was revealed, a man would divorce his wife and take her back many times, in some cases more than a hundred times, in order to be vengeful and cruel. However, Allah stated that this can be only done twice, and the third time it is final to protect the wife from harm.

If the divorce is to proceed, the husband is not permitted to take back the Mahr (dowry), unless she commits open illegal sexual intercourse [Verse 4.19] upon which the husband can take the Mahr back. Also, if the wife wants the divorce for no valid reason, then the husband can take the Mahr[ccxxvii]. Regarding this, Prophet Muhammad said:

"Any woman who asks her husband for divorce without justification, then the scent of Paradise will be forbidden for her."[ccxxviii]

If the wife gives the dowry back of her own accord, there is no sin on her for giving it back and there is no sin on the husband for accepting it.

After the third divorce, the man cannot take back this wife or remarry her. For that to happen, the woman must remarry another man and consummate the relationship and if her second husband divorces her, she is only then eligible to remarry her first husband.

However, this must be a genuine marriage; if the purpose of the second marriage of the woman is so that she becomes eligible for the first husband, this is unlawful and is called Tahlil – this has been cursed and criticized:

"Allah's Messenger [PBUH] cursed the one who does Tahlil, the one in whose favor it is done, those who eat Riba (usury) and those who feed it (pay the usury)."[ccxxix]

The Command to be Kind to the Divorced Wife

2.231 **And when you have divorced women and they have fulfilled the term of their prescribed period, either take them back on a reasonable basis or set them free on a reasonable basis. But do not take them back to hurt them, and whoever does that, then he has wronged himself. And treat not the Verses (Laws) of Allah in jest, but remember Allah's favors on you (i.e. Islam), and that which He has sent down to you of the Book (i.e. the Qur'an) and Al-Hikmah (the Prophet's Sunnah – legal ways – Islamic jurisprudence) whereby He instructs you. And fear Allah, and know that Allah is All-Aware of everything.**

When the divorce is final, Allah Commands the man to treat his wife with kindness, with no fighting or disputing, and he should ask her to depart from his house.

In addition, Allah Commands the man not to hurt the woman by divorcing her and just before her 'Iddah period was about to end, he would take her back; then he would divorce her and again, just before her 'Iddah period was about to end, he would again take her back. Allah prohibited this practice.[ccxxx]

The Command to the Wali of the Divorced Woman – Do not prevent her going back to her husband

2.232   **And when you have divorced women and they have fulfilled the term of their prescribed period, do not prevent them from marrying their (former) husbands, if they mutually agree on reasonable basis. This (instruction) is an admonition for him among you who believes in Allah and the Last Day. That is more virtuous and purer for you. Allah knows and you know not.**

The above Verse was revealed about a man called Ma'qil bin Yasar during the time of Prophet Muhammad [PBUH]. Ma'qil gave his sister in marriage to a man; however, after a while he divorced her and did not take her back until her 'Iddah had finished. She went back to her brother, Ma'qil. Her husband then desired for his wife again and she also wanted to marry him again. However, when he spoke to Ma'qil, he refused to grant his wish and vowed that he would never marry his sister. Allah then revealed the above Verse. When Ma'qil heard the above Verse he permitted his sister to marry her husband again.[ccxxxi] It was also said that Ma'qil paid the expiation for breaking his vow.[ccxxxii]

Rulings on the Suckling Period

2.233 **The mothers should suckle their children for two whole years, (that is) for those (parents) who desire to complete the term of suckling, but the father of the child shall bear the cost of the mother's food and clothing on a reasonable basis. No person shall have a burden laid on him greater than he can bear. No mother shall be treated unfairly on account of her child, nor father on account of his child. And on the (father's) heir is incumbent the like of that (which was incumbent on the father). If they both decide on weaning, by mutual consent, and after due consultation, there is no sin on them. And if you decide on a foster suckling-mother for your children, there is no sin on you, provided you pay (the mother) what you agreed (to give her) on reasonable basis. And fear Allah and know that Allah is All-Seer of what you do.**

The reason for not suckling the child after the 2nd year is so that the child is not harmed in body or mind.

Allah also states that Fitam (weaning) before the 2nd year requires mutual consent between the mother and father and one parent is not permitted to make this decision on their own. This is to protect the child's interests.

Regarding rearing the child, if the mother and father are both in agreement that the father has custody of the child (before the suckling period ends), then there is no sin on either of them. The father should compensate the mother for the period she suckled the child and should then seek to find a foster-mother to suckle the child.[ccxxxiii]

However, the mother should not turn down the offer to suckle the child just to hurt the father; conversely, the father is not permitted to take the child away from the mother just to harm the mother.

Ruling on the 'Iddah (waiting period) of the Widow

2.234   And those of you who die and leave wives behind them, they (the wives) shall wait (as regards their marriage) for four months and ten days, then when they have fulfilled their term, there is no sin on you if they (the wives) dispose of themselves in a (just and) honorable manner (i.e. they can marry). And Allah is Well-Acquainted with what you do.

If her husband dies, the widow's 'Iddah (waiting period before she can remarry) is four months and ten days.

Why did Allah legislate an 'Iddah period exactly this long? The reason is that the widowed woman may be pregnant as is explained in the following hadith:

> *"(The creation of) a human being is put together in the womb of his mother in forty days in the form of a seed . . ."[ccxxxiv]*

Hence, the fetus will shows signs of life after the soul has been breathed into it during this period.

If the widowed woman is pregnant, her 'Iddah period ends as soon as she gives birth, even if she gives birth straight after her husband dies (Verse 65.4).

Regarding whether the widowed woman is free or a slave, the 'Iddah period is exactly the same.[ccxxxv]

Mourning during the 'Iddah period for the deceased husband

Mourning the dead husband is required until the 'Iddah period has ended. Prophet Muhammad said:

> *"It is not lawful for a woman who believes in Allah and the Last Day to mourn for more than three days for any dead person except her husband, for whom she mourns for four months and ten days."[ccxxxvi]*

The Ruling on Marriage Proposals During the 'Iddah

2.235   **And there is no sin on you if you make a hint of betrothal or conceal it in yourself, Allah knows that you will remember them, but do not make a promise (of contract) with them in secret except that you speak an honorable saying. And do not be determined on the marriage bond until the term prescribed is fulfilled. And know that Allah knows what is in your minds, so fear Him. And know that Allah is Oft-Forgiving, Most Forbearing.**

The above Verse states that if a woman is in her 'Iddah period, a suitor may make a hint of marriage: "This means saying: 'I want to marry and I am looking for a woman whose qualities are such and such,' thus talking to her in general terms in a way that is better."[ccxxxvii] "A man can also say: 'I wish that Allah endows me with a wife,' but he should not make a direct marriage proposal."[ccxxxviii]

A man may also approach her Wali and say 'do not give her away (in marriage) until you inform me first.'[ccxxxix]

However, one is not permitted to say to a woman in her 'Iddah period that 'I am in love with you,' or 'promise me you will not marry someone else (after the 'Iddah finishes),' and so forth.[ccxl]

As a result of the above, it is agreed amongst the scholars that if there is a marriage contract during the 'Iddah period, they are invalid.

The Ruling on Divorce Before Consummating the Marriage Before Dowry is Agreed

2.236   There is no sin on you, if you divorce women while yet you have not touched (had sexual relation with) them, nor appointed unto them their due dowry. But give them a Mut'ah (a suitable gift), the rich according to his means, and the poor according to his means, a gift of reasonable amount is a duty on the doers of good.

The purpose of the gift (Mut'ah) is to compensate the woman for her loss.

The Ruling on Divorce Before Consummating the Marriage But After Dowry is Agreed

2.237   **And if you divorce them before you have touched (had a sexual relation with) them, and you have appointed for them their due (dowry), then pay half of that, unless they (the women) agree to remit it, or he (the husband), in whose hands is the marriage tie, agrees to remit it and giver her full appointed dowry. And to remit and give (her the full dowry) is nearer to At-Taqwa (piety, righteousness). And do not forget liberality between yourselves. Truly, Allah is All-Seer of what you do.**

It is important to note from the previous Verse [2.236], the above Verse is not a continuation of the Mut'ah (gift).

If the husband divorces the wife before the marriage is consummated, but after the dowry has been agreed, then Allah states that he must give her half of the appointed dowry.

However, the woman can forgo the half that she is entitled to.

The above Verse also states that it is better (more reward) if the husband gives the full amount of dowry agreed.

It is generally agreed that the Wali of the wife is not permitted to give away any of her rights without her consent, especially the dowry, as this belongs to her.

Command to Pray the Salah

2.238   **Guard strictly (five obligatory) As-Salawat (the prayers) especially the Middle Salah (i.e. the 'Asr Salah). And stand before Allah with obedience [and do not speak to others during the Salah (prayers)].**

2.239   **And if you fear (an enemy), (perform Salah) on foot or riding. And when you are in safety, then remember Allah (pray) in the manner He has taught you, which you knew not (before).**

Allah Commands His believing servants to offer the Salah: a companion asked Prophet Muhammad [PBUH]: 'Which deed is the dearest (to Allah)?' He replied:

"To offer the prayers at their fixed times."

After the Salah, the Prophet [PBUH] stated that the next best deed was Jihad in Allah's cause, followed by being good and dutiful to one's parents.[ccxli]

As the above Verse states, the 'Asr Salah is the best of the Salah and Allah has Commanded His believing servants generally to not miss the Salah, and more specifically, not to miss the 'Asr Salah. Prophet Muhammad [PBUH] said:

"Whoever misses the 'Asr prayer will be like who has lost his family and money."[ccxlii]

"On a cloudy day, perform the ('Asr) prayer early, for whoever misses the 'Asr prayer, will have his (good) deeds annulled."[ccxliii]

Allah also Commands you not to talk during the Salah as speaking contradicts the very nature of the prayer. Prophet Muhammad [PBUH] said:

"The ordinary speech people indulge in is not appropriate during the prayer. The prayer involves only Tasbih (praising Allah), Takbir (saying Allahu Akbar, i.e. saying Allah is the Most Great) and remembering Allah."[ccxliv]

The Fear Prayer

"If there is intense fear, pray on foot, riding, facing the Qiblah and otherwise."[ccxlv]

What should the believers pray during times of fear? "Allah has ordained the prayer by the words of your Prophet [PBUH]: four (Rakia) while residing, two Rak'ah while travelling and one Rak'ah during times of fear."

It has also been stated: "If the victory seems near and the Muslims are unable to perform the prayer (in the normal manner), they should pray by nodding each by himself. If they are unable to nod, they should delay the prayer until fighting is finished. When they feel safe, they should pray two Rak'ah. If they are unable, they should then pray one Rak'ah that includes two prostrations. If they are unable, then Takbir alone does not suffice, so they should delay the prayer until they are safe."[ccxlvi]

Allah states in the final part of the above Verse, during times of safety, prayer is performed as Allah has ordained, at the specified fixed times, with the complete bowing, prostration, standing, sitting and with attention both physically and devoting one's heart, in complete submission when supplicating to the Almighty.

The Abrogated Ayat

2.240   **And those of you who die and leave behind wives should bequeath for their wives a year's maintenance (and residence) without turning them out, but if they (wives) leave, there is no sin on you for that which they do of themselves, provided it is honorable (e.g. lawful marriage). And Allah is All-Mighty, All-Wise.**

This Verse was abrogated by Verse 2.234, which stated: ". . . they (the wives) shall wait (as regards their marriage) for four months and ten days."

2.241   **And for divorced women, maintenance (should be provided) on reasonable (scale). This is a duty on Al-Muttaqin (the pious).**

2.242   **Thus Allah makes clear His Ayat (Laws) to you, in order that you may understand.**

The Story of the Dead People

   2.243   **Did you (O Muhammad [PBUH]) not think of those who went forth from their homes in the thousands, fearing death? Allah said to them: "Die". And then He restored them to life. Truly, Allah is full of Bounty to mankind, but most men thank not.**

We begin with the story of the Dead People:

There were a people who lived in a city where the weather did not suit them. Consequently, an epidemic broke out and the conditions became so incredibly harsh that it evolved into a full plague. The survivors, numbering 4,000, fled their city and took refuge in the wilderness. They continued to travel from one area to the next until they came across a fertile valley. They found it pleasant enough and settled there.

Then Allah caused them to die as is described in the Qur'an: "Did you (O Muhammad) not think of those who went forth from their homes in thousands, fearing death? Allah said to them, "Die" . . ." [2:243]

Allah sent two angels to them, one from lower side of the valley and the other from the upper side of the valley. The two angels screamed in unison and the people died instantly.

Following their death, the people were moved to a different place where their bodies began to rot and disintegrate. When new people settled in that area, they built graves around them.

Many, many years later one of the Prophets of Allah passed by the dead people; his name was Hizqil, known as Ezekiel in the Bible and Tawrah.

Hizqil noticed the putrid corpses of the people who had died and he asked Allah to bring them back to life. Allah accepted his supplication and commanded him to say: 'O bones, Allah commands you to be covered with flesh, nerves and skin.'

The bones of each person were brought together, followed by the flesh, followed by the nerves and the skin.

Hizqil [AS] watched as Allah brought them back to life as is described in the latter part of the above Verse: ". . . And then He restored them to life. Truly, Allah is full of Bounty to mankind, but most men thank not." [2:243]

The people looked about themselves and at each other and proclaimed: 'All praise is due to You (O Allah!) and there is no deity worthy of worship except You.'

Regarding the plague, Prophet Muhammad [PBUH] said:

"If it (the plague) breaks out in a land that you are in, do not leave that land to escape from it. If you hear about it in a land, do not enter it."[ccxlvii]

Abandoning Jihad Does Not Alter Destiny

2.244   And fight in the Way of Allah and know that Allah is All-Hearer, All-Knower.

Allah states that performing Jihad (fighting in the cause of Allah) does not alter destiny; a person will not live longer if he does not perform Jihad for each and every single person's life span has been written before the first man was Created by the Almighty.

Just before he died, Khalid bin Al-Walid, the commander of the Muslim armies and who was known as the 'Sword of Islam', said: "I have participated in so-and-so number of battles. There is not a part of my body, but suffered a shot (of an arrow), a stab (of a spear) or a strike (of a sword). Yet, here I am, I die on my bed just as the camel dies! May the eyes of the cowards never taste sleep." He was sad because he died on his bed and not as a martyr![ccxlviii]

The Good Loan

2.245   **Who is he that will lend to Allah a goodly loan so that He may multiply it to him many times? And it is Allah that decreases or increases (your provisions), and unto Him you shall return.**

Allah Commands the His servants to spend in His cause for Allah will multiply his deeds. This is a recurring topic throughout the Qur'an.

The Story of the Jews who Sought a King to be Appointed Over Them

2.246   **Have you not thought about the group of the Children of Israel after (the time of) Musa? When they said to a Prophet of theirs: "Appoint for us a king and we will fight in Allah's Way." He said: "Would you then refrain from fighting, if fighting was prescribed for you?" They said: "Why should we not fight in Allah's way while we have been driven out of our homes and our children (families have been taken as captives)?" But when fighting was ordered for them, they turned away, all except a few of them. And Allah is All-Aware of the Zalimin (polytheists and wrong-doers).**

Allah gave Musa the Tawrah and the Tabut (the Ark of the Covenant) to give to the people. The Children of Israel kept hold of them, generation after generation, and as long as they had the Tawrah and the Tabut with them, anyone who fought them would suffer defeat. The main threat to their existence was not an invasion from opposing armies, but from the demons inside themselves; whenever they suffered hardship and prayed to Allah, they were saved. But, as was the custom with the Children of Israel, it was not long before they rebelled and disobeyed Allah by crafting idols and worshipping them and offering sacrifices to them.

There came a time when they were so far away from the right path that Allah allowed a king to overpower them; he took the Tabut and the Tawrah from them during battle[ccxlix]. Those who had memorized the Tawrah and who survived the battle were few in number.

With the Tawrah and the Tabut no longer with them, the Children of Israel suffered defeat after defeat against their powerful enemies; many of them were captured and they lost huge swathes of their land.

Allah sends Prophet Shamwil to aid the Children of Israel

Prophethood had been halted amongst the Children of Israel; only a pregnant woman remained of the offspring of Lavi in whom the Prophethood still appeared. The pregnant woman's husband had been killed and the rabbis kept her hidden so that she could give birth to a Prophet who would save them from suffering defeats and hardship and to guide them to Allah. The pregnant woman also invoked Allah and when she gave birth to a boy, she named him Shamwil (known in the Bible and Tawrah as Samuel).

Allah raised Shamwil to be a righteous person and when he reached the age of Prophethood, Allah Commanded him to call the people to worship Allah.

The people were disrespectful towards him and asked him to appoint a king from amongst themselves; their reasoning was that they would unite under the new king and destroy their enemies.

2.247 **And their Prophet (Shamwil) said to them: "Indeed Allah has appointed Talut (Saul) as a king over you." They said: "How can he be a king over us when we are fitter than him for the kingdom, and he has not been given enough wealth." He said: "Verily, Allah has chosen him above you and has increased him abundantly in knowledge and stature. And Allah grants His kingdom to whom He wills. And Allah is All-Sufficient for His creatures' needs, All-Knower."**

Shamwil appointed Talut as king over them; however, they did not want to accept him as he did not have enough wealth and was not as high ranked as some of the people felt they were.

The reason that the Israelites did not accept Talut as their king was because they thought of him as inferior to them. He was not a descendant of the house of kings among them, which had been from the offspring of Yahudha (known in the Bible and Torah as Judah), and instead it has been stated that he was from the progeny of Benjamin. As to his occupation, there is a difference of opinion; some said he was a water-carrier and brought water to the people whilst others said he dyed skins.

Instead of obeying their Prophet, the Israelites continued to defy him. Shamwil stated to them that it was not he who had chosen the king; this was a direct Command from Allah who had accepted their request to appoint a king over them. Shamwil stated his qualities to the people as is described in the above Verse.

2.248 **And their Prophet (Shamwil) said to them: Verily! The sign of His kingdom is that there shall come to you At-Tabut (a wooden box), wherein is Sakinah (peace and reassurance) from your Lord and a remnant of that which Musa and Harun (Aaron) left behind, carried by the angels. Verily, in this is a sign for you if you are indeed believers.**

The story of the one who took the ark and what happened to them is worth retelling here.

Who took the Ark? It has been claimed that it was the Philistines who captured it from the Children of Israel; upon victory, they took it back to their home city and placed it beside their idol, who was named Dagon. When they arose the following morning and went to visit their idol, they found that it had fallen face down before the ark. They placed him back in his place beside the ark; however, by the following morning it had again fallen face down before the ark. They realized that it was the work of Allah whom the Children of Israel had been commanded to follow but who had deviated from that path. The Philistines moved the ark from city to city. However, they were afflicted by tumors in their necks. As they moved it, the tumors began affecting every city that it was moved to and as a result their people were constantly in a state of panic. At last they decided to return it back to the Children of Israel.

How the Tabut was given to the people has been described as follows:

"The angels came down while carrying the Tabut between the sky and the Earth, until they placed it before Talut while the people were watching."[ccl]

When the people saw the Tabut being brought to Talut before their very eyes, they believed in him and accepted Talut as their king.

2.249   **Then when Talut (Saul) set out with the army, he said: "Verily, Allah will try you by a river. So whoever drinks thereof, he is not of me, and whoever tastes it not, he is of me, except him who takes (thereof) in the hollow of his hand." Yet, they drank thereof, all, except a few of them. So when he had crossed it (the river), he and those who believed with him, they said: "We have no power this day against Jalut (Goliath) and his hosts." But those who knew with certainty that they were to meet their Lord, said: "How often a small group overcame a mighty host by Allah's Leave?" And Allah is with As-Sabirin (the patient).**

We now move to the story where Talut takes his army to confront a powerful foe.

Talut took his army, which was huge and numbered 80,000[ccli], and marched forward until they reached a river. It was stated that it was the Shari'ah River, which flowed between Jordan and Palestine[cclii]. Others have said it was the River Jordan. On the other side of the river was their enemy whom they were commanded to fight.

Before crossing the river, Talut advised his people not to drink from the water.

The meaning of the above Verse is that the Israelites who remained with Talut were few in number as the vast majority ran away before the fighting even commenced; it has been claimed that those who remained behind numbered about 300 from the original 80,000. The 300 who had stayed behind thought that if they had larger numbers they would be victorious. However, Allah stated that victory comes from Him and Him alone, not from large numbers or a vast amount of military equipment.

It has been claimed that when the people saw the large numbers of the enemy, including the dreaded and very powerful Jalut (known in the Bible and Torah as 'Goliath'), they were extremely anxious. However, there were strong believers amongst them who stated, 'How often a small group overcame a mighty host by Allah's leave?' As a result, Allah assisted them in their battle.

On a final note on this part, Talut promised his people that the one killed the dreaded Jalut would be given his daughter's hand in marriage and therefore would have a share in his kingship. He was to keep his promise.

2.250   **And when they advanced to meet Jalut (Goliath) and his forces, they invoked: "Our Lord! Pour forth on us patience, and set firm our feet and make us victorious over the disbelieving people."**

2.251   So they routed them by Allah's Leave and Dawud (David) killed Jalut (Goliath), and Allah gave him (Dawud) the kingdom [after the death of Talut and Shamwil] and Al-Hikmah (Prophethood), and taught him of that which He willed. And if Allah did not check one set of people by means of another, the earth would indeed be full of mischief. But Allah is full of Bounty to the 'Alamin (mankind, Jinn and all that exists).

2.252   These are the Verses of Allah, We recite them to you (O Muhammad [PBUH]) in truth, and surely, you are one of the Messengers (of Allah).

When the Israelites saw the dreaded Jalut and his powerful army they prayed to Allah for help. Allah accepted their prayer and made them victorious as Allah states in the Qur'an.

The encounter between Dawud [AS] and Jalut has been described as follows:

"When Jalut challenged Talut to come forwards and fight him, and said: 'Will you come to me or shall I come to you?' No one had the courage to take up this challenge. So Talut announced among people that whoever should kill Jalut, he will marry him his daughter. Dawud came forward and took up the challenge, and killed Jalut." [ccliii]

In Ibn Kathir's tafsir of the Qur'an, it is stated that the Israelite accounts state that Dawud killed Jalut with a slingshot which he launched at him.

As soon as he had killed Jalut, Dawud instantly became a hero to the Israelites and they loved him. Talut abdicated the throne and the people replaced him with Dawud. Hence, kingship was transferred from Talut to Dawud, along with the Prophethood that Allah had granted him. It was the first time that both Prophethood and kingship came together in one family[ccliv].

Allah Judges The Messenger, Not Humans

2.253   **Those Messengers! We preferred some to others; to some of them Allah spoke (directly); others He raised to degrees (of honor); and to 'Isa, the son of Maryam, We gave clear proofs and evidences, and supported him with Ruh-il-Qudus (Jibril). If Allah had willed, succeeding generations would not have fought against each other, after clear Verses of Allah had come to them, but they differed - some of them believed and others disbelieved. If Allah had willed, they would not have fought against one another, but Allah does what He wills.**

Which Messengers did Allah speak to directly? To Adam, Musa and Muhammad [PBUH][cclv].

And Allah states that He has raised the Prophets to different ranks which is supported when Prophet Muhammad [PBUH] went on the Isra' (Night) journey and saw Prophets in the different levels of Heavens.

However, it is not up to us, the creation, to judge and decide with Prophet is better; this is Allah's decision and His alone. Prophet Muhammad [PBUH] said:

> *"Don't give me superiority above the Prophets, for the people will become unconscious on the Day of Resurrection, and I will be the first to be resurrected to see Musa holding on to the pillar of Allah's Throne. I will not know whether the unconsciousness Musa suffered on the Day of the Trumpet sufficed for him, or if he got up before me. So do not give me superiority above the Prophet."[cclvi]*

The Command to Spend in Allah's Cause

2.254   **O you who believe! Spend of that with which We have provided for you, before a Day comes when there will be no bargaining, nor friendship, nor intercession. And it is the disbelievers who are the Zalimin (wrong-doers).**

Allah Commands His servants to spend for His sake, in righteousness, before the Day of Resurrection which no one will be able to bargain out of, nor rely on friends or intercessors. Each person will be responsible for his or her actions whilst they were on earth.

Ayat Al-Kursi

2.255 **Allah! La ilaha illa Huwa (none has the right to be worshipped but He), the Ever Living, the One Who sustains and protects all that exists. Neither slumber, nor sleep overtake Him. To Him belongs whatever is in the heavens and whatever is on earth. Who is he that can intercede with Him except with His permission? He knows what happens to them (His creatures) in this world, and what will happen to them in the Hereafter. And they will never compass anything of His Knowledge except that which He wills. His Kursi extends over the heavens and the earth, and He feels no fatigue in guarding and preserving them. And He is the Most High, the Most Great.**

Ayat Al-Kursi has been described as the greatest Ayah in the Qur'an.

When Prophet Muhammad [PBUH] asked one of the Muslims what was the greatest Ayah in the Qur'an and he replied Ayat Al-Kursi, he said:

> *"Congratulations for having knowledge. By He in Whose Hand is my soul! This Ayah has a tongue and two lips with which she praises the King (Allah) next to the leg of the Throne."cclvii*

He also said:

> *"Allah's Greatest Name, if He was supplicated with it, He answers the supplication, is in three Surahs – Al-Baqarah, Al-Imran and Ta-Ha."cclviii*

These Verses are 2:255, 3:1-2 and 20:111, and Allah's Greatest Name has been described as: "The Ever Living, the One Who sustains and protects all that exists."

There are 10 individual sentences in Ayat Al-Kursi:

1. "Allah! None has the right to be worshipped but He"
   Means only Allah is worthy of worship.

2. "Al-Hayyul-Qayyum (the Ever Living, the One Who sustains and protects all that exists)"
   Means Allah is Ever Living, Who never dies, and Who sustains and protects everything that exists.

3. "Neither slumber nor sleep overtakes Him"
   Means that Allah does not sleep or slumber, hence He is aware of everything. Prophet Muhammad [PBUH] said:

"Allah does not sleep, and it does not befit His majesty that He sleeps. He lowers the scales and raises them. The deeds of the day are resurrected in front of Him before the deeds of the night, and the deeds of the night before the deeds of the day. His Veil is light, or fire, and if He removes it, the rays from His Face would burn whatever His sight reaches of His creation."[cclix]

4. "To Him belongs whatever is in the heavens and whatever is on the earth"
   Means that everyone is a servant of Allah, and everything belongs to Allah.

5. "Who is he that can intercede with Him except with His permission"
   Means that no one will be able to come to another person's aid on the Day of Resurrection, except if he is permitted by Allah. Prophet Muhammad stated:

   "I will stand under the Throne and fall in prostration, and Allah will allow me to remain in that position as much as He wills. I will thereafter be told: 'Raise your head, speak and you will be heard, intercede and your intercession will be accepted.'" The Prophet [PBUH] then said: *"He will allow me a proportion whom I will enter into Paradise."*[cclx]

6. "He knows what happens to them (His creatures) in this world, and what will happen to them in the Hereafter"
   Means that Allah knows everything that happens to His creatures; that includes everyone's past, present and their future.

7. "And they will never compass anything of His Knowledge except that which He wills"
   Means that no one is able to attain any knowledge of the Almighty, except what Allah wills to be known to that person.

8. "His Kursi extends over the heavens and the earth"
   It is stated that the "Kursi is the footstool, and no one is able to give due consideration to (Allah's) Throne."[cclxi]
   The Kursi is so vast that the it extends over the heavens and the earth; it has been stated that "if the seven heavens and the seven earths were flattened and laid side by side, they would add up to the size of a ring in a desert, compared to the Kursi."[cclxii]

9. "And He feels no fatigue in guarding and preserving them"
   Means that Allah does not get tired in protecting and preserving the heavens and the earth, and does not get tired in knowing about, sustaining and protecting everything in and between the heavens and the earths.

10. "And He is the Most High, the Most Great"
    Means Allah is the greatest

Command Not to Force People to Become Muslims

2.256   **There is no compulsion in religion. Verily, the right path has become distinct from the wrong path. Whoever disbelieves in Taught and believes in Allah, then he has grasped the most trustworthy handhold that will never break. And Allah is All-Hearer, All-Knower.**

The above Verse was revealed about the Ansar before the coming of Islam: "When (an Ansar) woman would not bear children who would live, she would vow that if she gives birth to a child who remains alive, she would raise him as a Jew. When Banu An-Nadir (the Jewish tribe) were evacuated (from Al-Madinah), some of the children of the Ansar were being raised among them, and the Ansar said: 'We will not abandon our children.'" Allah then revealed the above Verse.[cclxiii]

The above Verse states that there is no need to force people to convert to Islam because the religion of Islam is readily apparent; it is the right path and all other religions are the wrong path, and if Allah instills the light of faith in a person, nothing will deter him from following Allah.

In the above Verse, where it says Taghut, it means Shaytan.

In addition, where the Verse states: "grasped the most trustworthy handhold that will never break", this means Iman (faith)[cclxiv] or Islam[cclxv].

Only Allah Brings People into the Light

2.257   **Allah is the Wali (Protector or Guardian) of those who believe. He brings them out from darkness into light. But as for those who disbelieve, their Awliya' (supporters and helpers) are Taghut (false deities and false leaders), they bring them out from light into darkness. Those are the dwellers of the Fire, and they will abide therein forever.**

In the above Verse, Allah states that only He is the One who guides people from darkness to the light, meaning Islam and Paradise.

Allah also stated above: "But as for those who disbelieve, their Awliya' are Taghut, they bring them out from light into darknesses"; Allah has mentioned light in the singular, which means that there is only one straight path to Allah; however, Allah mentioned darkness in the plural, because although there is only one straight path, there are many, many paths that are false and lead to disbelief. This is something that is mentioned in the Qur'an again and again.

The Dispute Between Ibrahim and King Nimrod

2.258   **Have you not looked at him who disputed with Ibrahim (Abraham) about his Lord (Allah), because Allah had given him the kingdom? When Ibrahim said (to him): "My Lord (Allah) is He Who gives life and causes death." He said: "I give life and cause death." Ibrahim said: "Verily! Allah brings the sun from the east; then bring it you from the west." So the disbeliever was utterly defeated. And Allah guides not the people, who are Zalimin (wrong-doers, etc.).**

During the time of Ibrahim there were 4 kings who ruled over the Earth. Of these, two were believers who were called Dhul-Qarnayn and Sulayman bin Dawud (who was also a Prophet). The two disbelievers were Nabuchadnezzar and Nimrod.[cclxvi]

The latter, King Nimrod, was from the progeny of Nuh's son, Sam, as was Ibrahim. Nimrod ruled for a long time, 400 years, and was evil, rebellious and was the most arrogant person of his time. As a result of him ruling his people for such a long time, he called himself god and forced his people to believe in his absolute power over all things, similar to god. To demonstrate his power, he controlled all supplies of food; the only method by which his people could get food to feed their families was for them to go to him with empty sacks and wait to be granted an audience, which was part of him convincing the people that only he, King Nimrod, could grant them sustenance.

Following the period when Allah saved Ibrahim [AS] from the fire, Ibrahim [AS] went to Nimrod to get food for his family. It was during this time that he had the famous altercation with Nimrod, which is described in the above Verse.

It is important to describe the above verse in detail. Allah states that He had given Nimrod the kingdom and he ruled for a long time, and instead of being grateful, he became so arrogant that he denied the existence of god.

Nimrod asked Ibrahim to produce proof that Allah exists; Ibrahim [AS] replied: "My Lord is He Who gives life and causes death."

To this, Nimrod replied arrogantly: "I give life and cause death." To prove this, Nimrod commanded his chiefs to bring two people to him:

> *"Two people were brought in front of him whom he wanted to kill. He then ordered one of them to be killed, and spared the life of the other, and so he claimed that he granted life to one of them and caused death to the other person."* [cclxvii]

This was a stupid claim by Nimrod; as the above Verse claims, it was Allah who had granted him the kingdom, and instead of being grateful for all the Allah had bestowed upon him, he denied the existence of Allah and claimed that he was the one who gave people life and death.

Ibrahim then said to Nimrod that Allah brought the sun from the East and if he was truthful, he should bring it from the West. What Ibrahim was referring to is that He who brings life and death controls the existence and creates whatever is in it, including controlling the planets and their movements. The sun rises every day from the East but if Nimrod was proclaiming himself to be god, then he should try bringing it from the West.

To this, the king had no reply and was utterly humiliated.

Nimrod was so embarrassed at the degradation that he had suffered at the hands of Ibrahim that when the latter left, Nimrod refused to give him any food provisions. Ibrahim returned home with his two empty sacks and when he rested he fell asleep.

When his wife, Sara, looked at the sacks they were full to the brim with the best quality of food and she began preparing the meal. When he awoke, Ibrahim asked her where the food came from; she replied that it was what he had brought back home with him. Ibrahim realized that it was given by Allah and prayed earnestly to thank the Almighty for his endless blessings.

As for Nimrod, he was to meet an ignominious end:

> Allah sent an angel to the king and commanded him to believe in Allah and Allah Alone; however, Nimrod flatly refused. The angel came again and commanded him but he was met with the same response. When the angel returned for the third time and was again met with a firm refusal, the angel asked Nimrod to gather his army and the angel would gather his people. At sunrise, the appointed time, Nimrod gathered his army and all his people and waited.
>
> Allah sent a huge army of mosquitos that were so vast in number that they shaded the sun. The mosquitos fell upon Nimrod's army and his people, eating their flesh and drinking their blood. The worst fate was left for Nimrod – one of the mosquitos entered his nose and ate him from the inside; the king was in such pain that he took a hammer and smashed it into his head and killed himself. [cclxviii]

The Story of 'Uzayr

2.259   Or like the one who passed by a town in ruin up to its roofs. He said: "How will Allah ever bring it to life after its death?" So Allah caused him to die for a hundred years, then raised him up (again). He said: "How long did you remain (dead)?" He (the man) said: "(Perhaps) I remained (dead) a day or part of a day." He said: "Nay, you have remained (dead) for a hundred years, look at your food and your drink, they show no change; and look at your donkey! And thus We have made of you a sign for the people. Look at the bones, how We bring them together and clothe them with flesh." When this was clearly shown to him, he said: "I know (now) that Allah is able to do all things."

The above Verse is about a man from the Children of Israel named 'Uzayr and the town it refers to was Jerusalem. It was destroyed by Nebuchadnezzar who butchered its people in cold savagery.

When 'Uzayr saw the city in ruins he asked: 'How will Allah ever bring it to life after its death?' Allah caused him to die. Then, slowly the Children of Israel who survived the attack by Nebuchadnezzar and had scattered to other regions began to move back into the city and about seventy years after the death of 'Uzayr, the city was rebuilt.

After being dead for a hundred years, Allah resurrected 'Uzayr. The first sense that was returned to him was his eyes so that he could firstly witness the city being built and secondly witness how Allah brought him back to life.

The reason why 'Uzayr thought that he had died for only a day or part of a day was because he died in the early part of the day and when he was resurrected a hundred years later, it was the latter part of the day, so he answered: 'Or part of a day.' But Allah informed him that he had died for a hundred years.

As for his food and drink, Allah caused them to remain as they were and they were not spoilt.

As for his donkey, this been described as: "'Uzayr observed the bones of his donkey, which were scattered all around him to his right and left, and Allah sent a wind that collected the bones from all over the area. Allah then brought every bone to its place, until they formed a full donkey made of fleshless bones. Allah then covered these bones with flesh, nerves, veins and skin. Allah sent an angel who blew life in the donkey's nostrils, and the donkey started to bray by Allah's leave."[cclxix]

When he saw these miraculous signs of resurrection, 'Uzayr proclaimed: 'I know (now) that Allah is able to do all things.'

Ibrahim and Bringing the Birds Back to Life

2.260   And (remember) when Ibrahim said: "My Lord! Show me how You give life to the dead." He (Allah) said: "Do you not believe?" He (Ibrahim) said: "Yes (I believe), but to be stronger in faith." He said: "Take four birds, then cause them to incline towards you (then slaughter them, cut them into pieces), and then put a portion of them on every hill, and call them, they will come to you in haste. And know that Allah is All-Mighty, All-Wise."

This has been described in the following hadith:

> *As he was commanded, Ibrahim caught four birds, slaughtered them, removed the feathers, tore the birds to pieces and mixed the pieces together. He then placed parts of these mixed pieces on four or seven hills. Ibrahim kept the heads of these birds in his hand.*
> *Next, Allah commanded Ibrahim to call the birds to him, and he did as Allah commanded him. Ibrahim witnessed the feathers, blood and flesh of these birds fly to each other, and the parts flew each to their bodies, until every bird came back to life and came walking at a fast pace towards Ibrahim, so that the example that Ibrahim was witnessing would become more impressive. Each bird came to collect its head from Ibrahim's hand, and if he gave the bird another head the bird refused to accept it. When Ibrahim gave each bird its own head, the head was placed on its body by Allah's leave and power."* [cclxx]

Everybody has doubts from time to time which attack the heart and the thoughts that Shaytan inspires. As a result of this, we should always remember Allah and praise Him for everything that he has bestowed upon us. As the above story highlights, resurrection will occur by Allah's leave and when everybody dies, their souls will be brought back to life and we will all have to face the harsh reality of the Day of Judgment.

Parable of the Reward of Spending in Allah's Cause

2.261   **The parable of those who spend their wealth in the way of Allah, is that of a grain (of corn); it grows seven ears, and each ear has a hundred grains. Allah gives manifold increase to whom He wills. And Allah is All-Sufficient for His creatures' needs, All-Knower.**

The above Verse states that Allah will multiply good deeds done for His sake from ten up to seven-hundred times, according to the sincerity of the person performing the deed. A man once gave a camel together with its bridle in the cause of Allah; Prophet Muhammad [PBUH] said to the man:

> *"On the Day of Resurrection, you will have seven hundred camels with their bridles."*[cclxxi]

Prophet Muhammad [PBUH] added in another hadith:

> *"Every good deed that the son of Adam performs will be multiplied ten folds, to seven hundred folds, to many other folds, to as much as Allah wills. Allah said: 'Except the fast, for it is for Me and I will reward for it. One abandons his food and desire in My sake.' The fasting person has two times of happiness; when he breaks his fast and when he meets his Lord."*[cclxxii]

Giving Charity and Reminding People is Forbidden

2.262   **Those who spend their wealth in the cause of Allah, and do not follow up their gifts with reminders of their generosity or with injury, their reward is with their Lord. On them shall be no fear, nor shall they grieve.**

2.263   **Kind words and forgiving of faults are better than Sadaqah (charity) followed by injury. And Allah is Rich (free of all wants) and He is Most-Forbearing.**

2.264   **O you who believe! Do not render in vain your Sadaqah (charity) by reminders of your generosity or by injury, like him who spends his wealth to be seen of men, and he does not believe in Allah, nor in the Last Day. His likeness is the likeness of a smooth rock on which is a little dust; on it falls heavy rain which leaves it bare. They are not able to do anything with what they have earned. And Allah does not guide the disbelieving people.**

In the above Verse, Allah states that those who give charity but then remind people of the fact that they gave the charity, will render their charity in vain. This includes those who give charity and boast of giving it away, for they are not doing this for Allah's sake, but for material benefit of this worldly life including building a reputation of being kind and generous. These people will nullify their charity and are actually committing a very serious sin: Prophet Muhammad [PBUH] said:

> *"Three persons whom Allah shall neither speak to on the Day of Resurrection nor look at nor purify, and they shall receive a painful torment: he who reminds (the people) of what he gives away, he who lengthens his clothes below the ankles and he who swears an oath while lying, to sell his merchandise."*[cclxxiii]

Those who give charity only for Allah's sake, their 'reward is with their Lord', meaning Allah Himself will reward them, and 'on them shall be no fear', meaning the Day of Resurrection, and 'nor shall they grieve', meaning the children they leave behind.

Where the above Verse states the parable of dust, what this means is that although the people who give charity and then remind people of this fact think that their deeds are plentiful and will garner huge rewards, these are in fact the specks of dust on the rock which are easily washed away and will count for nothing.

The Parable of Those Who Give Charity Seeking Only Allah's Pleasure

2.265   **And the parable of those who spend their wealth seeking Allah's pleasure while they in their own selves are sure and certain that Allah will reward them (for their spending in His cause), is that of a garden on a height; heavy rain falls on it and it doubles its yield of harvest. And if it does not receive heavy rain, light rain suffices it. And Allah is All-Seer of (knows well) what you do.**

In the above Verse, Allah provides a parable for those who give charity seeking only Allah's pleasure; it is as if they have a garden on a height above ground-level, and if heavy rains fall on it, it yields a bumper harvest; however, if light rain falls on it, it is still sufficient to provide a good harvest.

The Parable of Evil Deeds Nullifying Good Deeds

2.266   **Would any of you wish to have a garden with date-palms and vines, with rivers flowing underneath, and all kinds of fruits for him therein, while he is stricken with old age, and his children are weak (not able to look after themselves), then it is struck with a fiery whirlwind, so that it is burnt? Thus does Allah make clear His Ayat (proofs, evidences, verses) to you that you may give thought.**

The above Verse states that those who do good deeds but follow them up with evil deeds, their evil deeds will nullify their good deeds and when they die and then meet Allah on the Day of Resurrection, it will be too late for them! Hence, the Day when they will desperately need good deeds to save them from the Fire, there will be none.

In the parable above, the old man was too old and had no strength to replant his garden and his children are too young and weak to assist him. This will be the state of those who nullify their good deeds and their children will be of no help to them.

Prophet Muhammad [PBUH] used to supplicate with:

> *"O Allah! Make Your biggest provision for me when I am old in age and at the time my life ends."*[cclxxiv]

Command to Spend Money for Allah's Sake Earned Through Honest Means

2.267 O you who believe! Spend of the good things which you have (legally) earned, and of that which We have produced from the earth for you, and do not aim at that which is bad to spend from it, (though) you would not accept it save if you close your eyes and tolerate therein. And know that Allah is Rich (free of all needs), and worthy of all praise.

2.268 Shaytan threatens you with poverty and orders you to commit Fahsha (evil deeds) whereas Allah promises you forgiveness from Himself and bounty, and Allah is All-Sufficient for His creatures' needs, All-Knower.

2.269 He grants Hikmah to whom He wills, and he, to whom Hikmah is granted, is indeed granted abundant good. But none remember (will receive admonition) except men of understanding.

Allah Commands His believing servants to give charity which is earned through honest and legal means.

The above Verse was revealed about the Ansar (local inhabitants who lived in Madinah during the time of Prophet Muhammad's [PBUH] emigration from Makkah to Madinah). They used to harvest date-trees and when they ripened they would hang them between two pillars so that those who had immigrated from Makkah, many of whom had no means to support themselves, could take. However, some of the Ansar would hang dates that had either not ripened or ones that they did not want to eat themselves. As a result, Allah revealed: 'and do not aim at that which is bad to spend from it.'

Allah states that 'Shaytan threatens you with poverty', meaning that Shaytan tells the people that by spending in Allah's cause, they will become poor, and instead Shaytan tells the people to commit Fahsha, meaning all kinds of evil deeds.

However, Allah states that He promises the people that by obeying Him and His Commands, they will earn His forgiveness and He will provide them with bounty both in this life and in the Hereafter.

What does Hikmah mean? It means 'knowledge of the Qur'an. For instance, the abrogating and the abrogated, what is plain and clear and what is not as plain and clear, what it allows, and what it does not allow, and its parables'.[cclxxv] And those who have acquired Hikmah, through the will of Allah, he is indeed granted good which will lead to Paradise. Prophet Muhammad [PBUH] said:

"There is no envy except in two instances: a person whom Allah has endowed with wealth and he spends it righteously, and a person whom Allah has given Hikmah and he judges by it and teaches it to others."[cclxxvi]

The Ruling on When Disclosing Sadaqah is Permitted

2.270 **And whatever you spend for spendings (e.g., in Sadaqah – in charity for Allah's sake) or whatever vow you make, be sure Allah knows it all. And for the Zalimin (wrong-doers) there are no helpers.**

2.271 **If you disclose your Sadaqat (alms-giving), it is well; but if you conceal it and give it to the poor, that is better for you. (Allah) will expiate you some of your sins. And Allah is Well-Acquainted with what you do.**

In the above Verse, Allah states that He knows fully what each person gives in charity and for what purpose (i.e. for Allah's sake or for worldly gain) and He will reward accordingly.

Allah also states that it is better to conceal giving charity as it prevents one from boasting, however, one is permitted to disclose giving charity if there is a real benefit, for example, a person gives to encourage others to give, but it still has to be for Allah's sake and the person must not show or feel any level of being proud or want acclaim from others. Prophet Muhammad [PBUH] said:

> "He who utters aloud Qur'anic recitation is just like he who discloses charity acts. He who conceals Qur'anic recitation is just like he who conceals charity acts."[cclxxvii]

In summary, it is better to give charity without disclosing it; Prophet Muhammad [PBUH] said:

> "Allah will give shade to seven on the Day when there will be no shade but His. (They are): 1. A just ruler; 2. A youth who has been brought up in the worship of Allah; 3. Two persons who love each other only for Allah's sake who meet and part in Allah's cause only; 4. A man whose heart is attached to the Masjids from the time he departs the Masjid until he returns to it; 5. A person who remembers Allah in seclusion and his eyes are then flooded with tears; 6. A man who refuses the call of a charming woman of noble birth for illicit intercourse with her and says: 'I fear Allah, Lord of the worlds'; and 7. A man who gives charitable gifts so secretly that his left hand does not know what his right hand has given."[cclxxviii]

Allah adds in the above Verse that by giving charity, particularly one that is concealed, He will forgive some of your sins.

The Ruling on Giving Charity to Disbelievers

2.272 Not upon you (Muhammad [PBUH]) is their guidance, but Allah guides whom He wills. And whatever you spend in good, it is for yourselves, when you spend not except seeking Allah's Face. And whatever you spend in good, it will be repaid to you in full, and you shall not be wronged.

2.273 (Charity is) for Fuqara' (the poor), who in Allah's cause are restricted (from travel), and cannot move about in the land (for trade or work). The one who knows them not, thinks that they are rich because of their modesty. You may know them by their mark, they do not beg of people at all. And whatever you spend in good, surely Allah knows it well.

2.274 Those who spend their wealth (in Allah's cause) by night and day, in secret and in public, they shall have their reward with their Lord. On them shall be no fear, nor shall they grieve.

The above Verse was revealed because the Muslims disliked giving charity to polytheists; however, when the above Verse was revealed, they were permitted to do so. It is stated: "You give away charity for the sake of Allah. Therefore, you will not be asked about the deeds (or wickedness) of those who receive it."[cclxxix] There is a hadith with explains this in detail, in which Prophet Muhammad [PBUH] said:

> "A man said: 'Tonight, I shall give charity.' He went out with his charity and (unknowingly) gave it to an adulteress. The next morning the people said that alms were given to an adulteress. The man said: 'O Allah! All the praises are for You. (I gave my alms) to an adulteress. Tonight, I shall give alms again.' He went out with his charity and (unknowingly) gave it to a rich person. The next morning (the people) said: 'Last night, a wealthy person was given alms.' He said: 'O Allah! All the praises are for You. (I gave alms) to a wealthy man. Tonight, I shall again give charity.' So he went out with his charity and (unknowingly) gave it to a thief. The next morning (the people) said: 'Last night, a thief was given alms.' He said: 'O Allah! All the praises are for You. (I have given alms) to an adulteress, a wealthy man and a thief.' Then, someone came to him and said: 'The alms that you gave away were accepted. As for the adulteress, the alms might make her abstain from adultery. As for the wealthy man, it might make him take a lesson and spend his wealth that Allah has given him. As for the thief, it might make him abstain from stealing.'"[cclxxx]

Those deserving of charity

Where the above Verse states: '(Charity is) for Fuqara' (the poor), who in Allah's cause are restricted (from travel),' this refers to the Muslims who emigrated from Makkah to Madinah and they did not have any or very minimal resources to support themselves.

Where the above Verse states: 'The one who knows them not, thinks that they are rich because of their modesty,' this means the people think they are rich because they are modest in both physical appearance and in speech.

And where the above Verse states: 'You may know them by their mark,' means that those who have sound understanding will know who they are.

And where the above Verse states: 'they do not beg of people at all,' Prophet Muhammad [PBUH] said:

> *"The Miskin (needy) is not he who wanders about and whose need is sufficed by a date or two, a bite or two or a meal or two. Rather, the Miskin is he who neither has enough resources to sustain him, all the while people are unaware of his need so they do not give to him, nor does he ask people for anything."*[cclxxxi]

This is explained further by the following hadith, in which Abu Sai'd said:

> *"My mother sent me to the Messenger of Allah [PBUH] to ask him for help, but when I came to him I sat down. The Prophet [PBUH] faced me and said to me:*
> *"Whoever felt satisfied, then Allah will enrich him. Whoever is modest, Allah will make him decent. Whoever is content, then Allah will suffice for him. Whoever asks people, while having a small amount, he will have begged the people."*
> *I (Abu Sa'id) said to myself: 'I have a camel, and indeed, it is worth more than a small amount.' And I went back without asking the Prophet [PBUH] for anything."*[cclxxxii]

Spending on one's family is also Sadaqah

Prophet Muhammad [PBUH] said:

> *"You will not spend charity with which you seek Allah's Face, but you will ascend a higher degree and status because of it, including what you put in your wife's mouth."*[cclxxxiii]

In another hadith, he said:

> *"When the Muslim spends on his family while awaiting the reward for it from Allah, it will be written as charity for him."*[cclxxxiv]

Command not to deal with Riba (interest and usury)

2.275   **Those who eat Riba (usury) will not stand (on the Day of Resurrection) except like the standing of a person beaten by Shaytan leading him to insanity. That is because they say: "Trading is only like Riba," whereas Allah has permitted trading and forbidden Riba. So whosoever receives an admonition from his Lord and stops eating Riba, shall not be punished for the past; his case is for Allah (to judge); but whoever returns (to Riba), such are the dwellers of the Fire – they will abide therein.**

Allah states in the above Verse that Riba (interest and usury) is strictly prohibited. Prophet Muhammad [PBUH] said:

> *"May Allah curse whoever consumes Riba, whoever pays Riba, the two who are witnesses to it, and the scribe who records it."*[cclxxxv]

The person who deals with Riba is described in the dream that the Prophet Muhammad [PBUH] had:

> *"We reached a river – the narrator said: 'I thought he said that the river was as red as blood' – and found that a man was swimming in the river, and on its bank there was another man standing with a large collection of stones next to him. The man in the river would swim, then come to the man who had collected the stones and open his mouth, and the other man would throw a stone in his mouth."* The man in the river was the one who consumed Riba.[cclxxxvi]

However, whoever was not aware that Riba was prohibited is pardoned, but as soon as he becomes aware of this, he must never return to it. When Makkah was conquered, Prophet Muhammad [PBUH] said:

> *"All cases of Riba during the time of Jahiliyyah (pre-Islamic period of ignorance) is annulled and under my feed, and the first Riba I annul is the Riba of Al-'Abbas (the Prophet's uncle)."*[cclxxxvii]

It is also important to note that there are many types of Riba and some are not as evidently clear as others. The best way to judge on these is to review the hadith quoted by 'Umar: "The Ayah about Riba was one of the last Ayah to be revealed, and the Messenger of Allah [PBUH] died before he explained it to us. So leave that which makes you doubt for that which does not make you doubt."[cclxxxviii]

Hence, it is best to stay clear of the actions and the means that lead to these actions; Prophet Muhammad [PBUH] added:

"Both lawful and unlawful things are evident, but in between them there are matters that are not clear. So whoever saves himself from these unclear matters, he saves his religion and his honor. And whoever indulges in these unclear matters, he will have fallen into the prohibitions, just like a shepherd who grazes (his animals) near a private pasture, at any moment he is liable to enter it."[cclxxxix]

Allah does not accept charity from Riba

2.276   **Allah will destroy Riba (usury) and will give increase for Sadaqat (deeds of charity, alms) And Allah likes not the disbelievers, sinners.**

2.277   **Truly those who believe, and do deeds of righteousness, and perform Salah and give Zakah, they will have their reward with their Lord. On them shall be no fear, nor shall they grieve.**

In the above Verse Allah states that He will destroy Riba, either by taking it away from those who eat it or removing any blessing from it and hence the money they earn and spend will not benefit them in this life or the Hereafter. It is stated that: 'Riba will end up with less, even if it was substantial.'[ccxc]

The reward for giving in charity from honest resources is higher in rank than those who give huge sums from dishonest sources such as Riba. Prophet Muhammad [PBUH] said:

"Whoever gives in charity what equals a date from honest resources, and Allah only accepts that which is good and pure, then Allah accepts it with His right (Hand) and raises it for its giver, just as one of you raises his animal, until it becomes as big as a mountain."[ccxci]

Those who deal with Riba can expect a war from Allah and His Messenger [PBUH]

2.278   **O you who believe! Have Taqwa (fear) of Allah and give up what remains (due to you) from Riba (usury) (from now onward), if you are (really) believers.**

2.279   **And if you do not do it, then take a notice of war from Allah and His Messenger but if you repent, you shall have your capital sums. Deal not unjustly (by asking more than your capital sums), and you shall not be dealt with unjustly (by receiving less than your capital sums).**

In the above Verses Allah states that you should fear Allah and do not take back anything that is owed to you if it involves Riba. And Allah states that those who do not heed the warnings of Riba, they should expect war from Allah and His Messenger. What this means is that: "Whoever kept dealing with Riba and did not refrain from it, then the Muslim Leader should require him to repent. If he still did not refrain from Riba, the Muslim Leader should cut off his head."[ccxcii]

Prophet Muhammad [PBUH] gave a speech during the Farewell Hajj in which he said:

"Verily, every case of Riba from Jahiliyyah is completely annulled. You will only take back your capital, without increase or decrease. The first Riba that I annul is the Riba of Al-'Abbas bin 'Abdul-Muttalib, all of it is annulled."[ccxciii]

Command to be Kind to Debtors

2.280 **And if the debtor is in a hard time (has no money), then grant him time till it is easy for him to repay; but if you remit it by way of charity, that is better for you if you did but know.**

The above Verses were revealed because during the time of Jahiliyyah, if a person was owed money, he would go to the debtor and demand payment, and if he could not pay, he would begin adding interest to it. Allah stated that it is better to give the debtor time to pay the money back; however, if the person is struggling to pay the money back, it is better to forfeit the money and cancel the debt for the sake of Allah. Prophet Muhammad [PBUH] said:

"Whoever gives time to a debtor facing hard times, will earn charity multiplied two times for each day he gives."[ccxciv]

Being kind to debtors is also a sure way to Paradise; Prophet Muhammad [PBUH] stated:

"On the Day of Resurrection, one of Allah's servants will be summoned before Him and He will ask him: 'What deeds did you perform for Me in your life?' He will say: 'O Lord! In my life, I have not performed a deed for Your sake that equals an atom,' three times. The third time, the servant will add: 'O Lord! You granted me wealth and I used to be a merchant. I used to be lenient, giving easy terms to those well-off and giving time to the debtors who faced hard times.' Allah will say: 'I Am the Most Worthy of giving easy terms. Therefore, enter Paradise.'"[ccxcv]

The Last Verse Revealed from The Qur'an

2.281   And have Taqwa (fear) the Day when you shall be brought back to Allah. Then every person shall be paid what he earned, and they shall not be dealt with unjustly.

Command to Documented Transactions (abrogated by Verse 2:283)

2.282 O you who believe! When you contract a debt for a fixed period, write it down. Let a scribe write it down in justice between you. Let not the scribe refuse to write as Allah has taught him, so let him write. Let him (the debtor) who incurs the liability dictate, and he must have Taqwa (fear) of Allah, his Lord, and diminish not anything of what he owes. But if the debtor is of poor understanding, or weak, or is unable to dictate himself, then let his guardian dictate in justice. And get two witnesses out of your own men. And if there are not two men (available), then a man and two women, such as you agree for witnesses, so that if one of them (two women) errs, the other can remind her. And the witnesses should not refuse when they are called (for evidence). You should not become weary to write it (your contract), whether it be small or big, for its fixed term, that is more just with Allah; more solid as evidence, and more convenient to prevent doubts among yourselves, save when it is a present trade which you carry out on the spot among yourselves, then there is no sin on you if you do not write it down. But take witnesses whenever you make a commercial contract. Let neither scribe nor witness suffer any harm, but if you do (such harm), it would be wickedness in you. So have Taqwa (fear) of Allah; and Allah teaches you. And Allah is the All-Knower of everything.

The above Verse is longest in the Qur'an.

In the above Verse Allah Commanded His believing servants to document transactions. However, this was abrogated in the next Verse which states: 'Then if one of you entrusts the other, let the one who is entrusted discharge his trust (faithfully).' [2:283]

Allah also states that if the transaction is to be fulfilled immediately, then there is no harm if it is not recorded.

Why did Allah state: 'And if there are not two men (available), then a man and two women.' This is because of the shortcomings in women. Prophet Muhammad [PBUH] said:

"O women! Give away charity and ask for forgiveness, for I saw that you comprise the majority of the people of the Fire."
A woman asked: "O Messenger of Allah! Why do we comprise the majority of the people of the Fire?"
He said: "You curse a lot and you do not appreciate your mate. I have never seen those who have shortcomings in mind and religion controlling those who have sound minds, other than you."
She said: "O Messenger of Allah! What is the shortcoming in mind and religion?"

He said: "As for the shortcoming in her mind, the testimony of two women equals the testimony of one man, and this is the shortcoming in the mind. As for the shortcoming in the religion, woman remains for nights at a time when she does not pray and breaks the fast in Ramadan."[ccxcvi]

Documenting Transactions is not obligatory in certain conditions

2.283 **And if you are on a journey and cannot find a scribe, then let there be a pledge taken (mortgaging); then if one of you entrusts the other, let the one who is entrusted discharge his trust (faithfully), and let him have Taqwa (fear) of Allah, his Lord. And conceal not the evidence for he, who hides it, surely, his heart is sinful. And Allah is All-Knower of what you do.**

The above Verse states that if you cannot find a scribe, then a pledge suffices. But "if you trust each other, then there is no harm if you do not write the loan or have witnesses present."[ccxcvii]

The responsibility of the debt lies with the debtor and he must give it back unless he is forgiven by the person he took it from. Prophet Muhammad [PBUH] said:

> "The hand (of the debtor) will carry the burden of what it took until it gives it back."[ccxcviii]

Giving evidence truthfully and honestly is a Command from Allah, even if it be against yourselves or your parents [Verse 4:135]. It is also stated that: "False testimony is one of the worst of the major sins, and such is the case with hiding the true testimony."[ccxcix]

The Believers are not held Accountable for what is in their hearts

2.284 **To Allah belongs all that is in the heavens and all that is on the earth, and whether you disclose what is in yourselves or conceal it, Allah will call you to account for it. Then He forgives whom He wills and punishes whom He wills. And Allah is Able to do all things.**

"When this Ayah was revealed, it was very hard on the Companions of the Messenger of Allah [PBUH] and worried them tremendously. They said: 'O Messenger of Allah! We know that we would be punished according to our statements and our actions, but as for what occurs in our hearts, we do not control what is in them.' The Messenger of Allah [PBUH] said: "Say: 'We hear and we obey.'
They said: 'We hear and we obey.'
Thereafter, this Ayah was abrogated by the following Verses [2:283 and 2:284].[ccc]

As a result, Muslims are not held accountable for what is in their hearts, they are only held accountable for their actions. Prophet Muhammad [PBUH] said:

"Allah has pardoned my Ummah for what they say to themselves, as long as they do not utter it or act on it."[ccci]

The Prophet [PBUH] also said:

"Allah said (to His angels): 'If My servant intends to commit an evil deed, do not record it as such for him, and if he commits it, write id for him as one evil deed. If he intends to perform a good deed, but did not perform it, then write it for him as one good deed, and if he performs it, write it for him as ten good deeds.'"[cccii]

The Virtue of the Last Two Verses of Surah Al-Baqarah

2.285 The Messenger believes in what has been sent down to him from his Lord, and (so do) the believers. Each one believes in Allah, His Angels, His Books, and His Messengers. (They say): "We make no distinction between one another of His Messengers" – and they say: "We hear, and we obey. (We seek) Your forgiveness, our Lord, and to You is the return (of all)."

2.286 Allah burdens not a person beyond his scope. He gets reward for that (good) which he has earned, and he is punished for that (evil) which he has earned. "Our Lord! Punish us not if we forget or fall into error, our Lord! Lay not on us a burden like that which You did lay on those before us (Jews and Christians); our Lord! Put not on us a burden greater than we have strength to bear. Pardon us and grant us Forgiveness. Have mercy on us. You are our Mawla (Patron, Supporter and Protector) and give us victory over the disbelieving people."

How and when the last Verse of Surah Al-Baqarah was revealed is described as follows: "When the Messenger of Allah [PBUH] went on the Isra (Night) Journey, he ascended to Sidrat Al-Munthaha in the 6th heaven . . . he was given three things: the Salah (five prayers), the last Ayah in Surah Al-Baqarah and forgiveness for whoever did not associate anything or anyone with Allah from his Ummah."[ccciii]

The virtues of the last Surah has been described as follows: "While the Messenger of Allah [PBUH] was with Jibril, he heard a noise from above. Jibril lifted his sight to the sky and said: 'This is a door that was opened just now in heaven, and it was never opened before.' An angel came down through the door to the Prophet [PBUH] and said: 'Receive the good news of two lights that you have been given and which no Prophet before you was given: the Opener of the Book (Al-Fatihah) and the last Ayah in Surah Al-Baqarah. You will not read a letter of them, but you will be granted its benefit."[ccciv]

Prophet Muhammad [PBUH] said:

> *"Whoever recites the last two Ayah in Surah Al-Baqarah at night, they will suffice for him."*[cccv]

What the above Verses confirm is that Allah will only punish a person for what one is able to protect himself from; however, such things as passing thoughts or what he says to himself, they will not be punished. This is a great blessing and a mercy from Allah.

It is also stated that whenever Mu'adh finished reciting this Surah, he would say: "Amin."[cccvi]

[i] Narrated by Sahl bin Sa'd and others, recorded by At-Tabarani and Ibn Hibban.

[ii] Narrated from 'Abdullah bin Buraydah, recorded by Imam Ahmad.

[iii] Narrated by Ibn Jarir, recorded by At-Tabari.

[iv] Narrated by Abu Al-'Aliyah and Qatadah bin Di'amah, recorded by At-Tabari.

[v] Narrated by Qatadah, recorded by Ibn Abi Hatim.

[vi] Narrated by Ibn 'Abbas, recorded by At-Tabari.

[vii] Recorded by At-Tabari.

[viii] Recorded by Abu Dawud.

[ix] Recorded by Ibn Abi Hatim.

[x] Narrated by Qatadah.

[xi] Narrated by Abu Hurayrah, recorded by At-Tirmidhi, An-Nassai and Ibn Majah.

[xii] Narrated by 'Umar bin Al-Khattab, recorded by Sahih Al-Bukhari and Sahih Muslim.

[xiii] Recorded by Sahih Muslim and Fath Al-Bari.

[xiv] Narrated by Qatadah, recorded by Ibn Abi Hatim.

[xv] Narrated by Abu Al-'Aliyah, Ar-Rabi' bin Anas and Qatadah, recorded by Ibn Abi Hatim.

[xvi] Narrated by Ibn Jarir, recorded by At-Tabari.

[xvii] Narrated by Ibn 'Abbas, recorded by At-Tabari.

[xviii] Narrated by Ibn Jarir.

[xix] Narrated by Qatadah, recorded by Ibn Abi Hatim.

[xx] Narrated by Ibn 'Abbas, recorded by At-Tabari.

[xxi] Narrated by 'Abdullah bin 'Amr, recorded by Sahih Muslim and Fath Al-Bari.

[xxii] Narrated by Abu Hurayrah, recorded by Sahih Muslim and Fath Al-Bari.

[xxiii] Recorded by Sahih Muslim.

[xxiv] Narrated by Ibn Mas'ud, recorded by Sahih Muslim.

[xxv] Narrated by Yahya bin Abi Kathir, recorded by Ibn Abi Hatim.

[xxvi] Narrated by 'Ikrimah, recorded by at-Tabari.

[xxvii] Recorded by At-Tabari.

[xxviii] Narrated by Ibn 'Abbas, Ibn Mas'ud and some Companions, recorded by At-Tabari.

[xxix] Narrated by Mujahid, recorded by Ibn Abi Hatim.

[xxx] Chapter 41, Verses 9-12; the details regarding the breakdown of the days are provided in the Tafsir of Ibn Kathir, in Volume 8 pages 516 to 523.

[xxxi] Al-Qurtubi and other scholars also.

[xxxii] Narrated by Ibn 'Abbas, recorded by At-Tabari.

[xxxiii] Narrated by Ibn 'Abbas, recorded by At-Tabari.

[xxxiv] This is confirmed in Surah 18, Verse 50 which states: "And (remember) when We said to the angels; "Prostrate to Adam." So they prostrated except Iblis (Satan). He was one of the jinns . . ."

[xxxv] Recorded by Sahih Muslim.

[xxxvi] Narrated by Mu'adh, recorded by At-Tirmidhi.

[xxxvii] Narrated by Abu Hurayrah, recorded in Musnad At-Tayalisi no. 332. Similar is recorded by Al-Bukhari without the addition of 'It is the Tree of Eternity'.

[xxxviii] Al-Qurtubi mentioned several beneficial Hadiths here about snakes and the ruling on killing them.

[xxxix] Narrated by Ubayy bin Ka'b, recorded by At-Tabari.

[xl] Recorded by At-Tabari.

[xli] Narrated by Ibn 'Abbas, recorded by Musnad At-Tayalisi.

[xlii] Narrated by 'Abdullah Ibn 'Abbas, recorded by At-Tabari.

[xliii] Narrated by Ibn Jurayj, recorded by At-Tabari.

[xliv] Narrated by Abu Wa'il, recorded by Imam Ahmad.

[xlv] Recorded by Al-Qurtubi.

[xlvi] Narrated by Ibn 'Abbas, recorded by At-Tabari.

[xlvii] Recorded by Sahih Muslim.

xlviii Narrated by Mu'awiyah bin Haydah Al-Qushayri, recorded by Imam Ahmad and Ibn Majah.

xlix Narrated by Ibn 'Abbas, recorded by At-Tabari.

l Narrated by Ibn 'Abbas, recorded by Sahih Al-Bukhari.

li The story of Samiri has been told in detail in Surah 20, Verses 95 to 98.

lii Narrated by Ibn 'Abbas, recorded by At-Tabari.

liii Narrated by Ibn Jarir, recorded by At-Tabari.

liv Narrated by Qatadah, recorded by Ibn Abi Hatim.

lv Narrated by Ibn 'Abbas, recorded by At-Tabari. This has also been stated by Mujahid, Ash-Sha'bi, Ad-Dahhak, Al-Hassan, 'Ikrimah and Ar-Rabi' bin Anas, and recorded by Ibn Abi Hatim.

lvi Narrated by 'Ikrimah, recorded by Ibn Abi Hatim.

lvii Narrated by Qatadah.

lviii Narrated by Ibn 'Abbas, recorded by At-Tabari.

lix Narrated by 'Abdullah bin Mas'ud, recorded by Imam Ahmad.

lx Explanation by Ibn 'Abbas.

lxi Verified by Abu Al-'Aliyah and Ar-Rabi', recorded by Ibn Abi Hatim.

lxii Narrated by Ibn 'Abbas, recorded by Ibn Abi Hatim.

lxiii Narrated by Qatadah, recorded by Ibn Abi Hatim.

lxiv Narrated by 'Ubaydah As-Salmani, recorded by Ibn Abi Hatim.

lxv Narrated by 'Ubaydah As-Salmani, recorded by Ibn Abi Hatim.

lxvi Narrated by 'Ubaydah As-Salmani, recorded by Ibn Abi Hatim.

lxvii Narrated by Anas b. Malik, recorded by Sahih Al-Bukhari, Sahih Muslim and Fath Al-Bari.

lxviii Recorded by Sahih Muslim.

lxix Narrated by Ibn Abbas, recorded by Jami at-Tirmidhi,

lxx Narrated by Qatadah, recorded by Ibn Abi Hatim.

lxxi Narrated by Mujahid, recorded by At-Tabari.

lxxii Narrated by Ibn Wahb, recorded by At-Tabari.

lxxiii Narrated by Ibn 'Abbas, recorded by At-Tabari.

lxxiv Narrated by Abu Hurayrah, recorded by Imam Ahmad, Sahih Al-Bukhari and An-Nasa'i.

lxxv Narrated by Abu Razin, recorded by Ibn Abi Hatim.

lxxvi Narrated by 'Abdullah bin Mas'ud, recorded by Imam Ahmad.

lxxvii Narrated by Ibn Mas'ud, recorded by Sahih Muslim and Fath Al-Bari.

lxxviii Narrated by Abu Dharr, recorded by Imam Ahmad.

lxxix Narrated by 'Aisha, recorded by Sahih Al-Bukhari.

lxxx Narrated by Ibn 'Abbas, recorded by At-Tabari.

lxxxi Narrated by Abu Al-'Aliyah, recorded by Ibn Abi Hatim.

lxxxii Narrated by Ibn 'Abbas, recorded by Al-Qurtubi.

lxxxiii Narrated by Abu Al-'Aliyah, recorded by Ibn Abi Hatim.

lxxxiv Narrated by 'Amr bin Shu'ayb, recorded by Imam Ahmad.

lxxxv Narrated by Ibn 'Abbas, recorded by Ibn Abi Hatim.

lxxxvi Narrated by Ibn 'Abbas, recorded by Ibn Abi Hatim.

lxxxvii Narrated by 'Abdur-Rahman bin Zayd bin Aslam, recorded by At-Tabari.

lxxxviii Recorded by At-Tabari.

lxxxix Narrated by Abu Hurayrah, recorded by Fath Al-Bari.

xc Narrated by Malik bin As-Sayf, recorded by At-Tabari.

xci Narrated by Al-Hasan Al-Basri, recorded by Ibn Abi Hatim.

xcii Narrated by As-Suddi, recorded by At-Tabari.

xciii Narrated by As-Suddi, recorded by At-Tabari.

xciv Narrated by 'Abdullah, recorded by Kashaf Al-Astar.

xcv Narrated by Jabir bin 'Abdullah, recorded by Sahih Muslim.

xcvi Narrated by Abu Dawud, recorded by Ibn Hibban (Bulugh al-Maram).

xcvii Recorded by Sahih Muslim.

xcviii Narrated by 'Umar bin Al-Khattab, recorded by At-Qurtubi.

xcix Narrated by Ibn Khuwayz Mindad Al-Maliki.

c Narrated by Abu Al-'Aliyah, recorded by At-Tabari.

ci Narrated by Mujahid, 'Ata', As-Suddi, Qatadah and Ar-Rabi' bin Anas, recorded by Ibn Abi Hatim.

cii Narrated by Jabir, recorded by Ibn Abi Hatim.

ciii Recorded by Tuhfat Al-Ahwadhi.

civ Narrated by 'Abdullah bin 'Abbas, recorded by Sahih Muslim and Fath Al-Bari.

cv Narrated by Jabir, recorded by Sahih Muslim.

cvi This hadith has been recorded by Al-Bukhari.

cvii Narrated by 'Abdullah bin 'Amr bin Al-'As, recorded by Imam Ahmad.

cviii Narrated by Abu Hurayrah, recorded by Sahih Muslim.

cix Narrated by Abu Dharr, recorded by Imam Ahmad.

cx Narrated by Abu Hurayrah, recorded by At-Tirmidhi, Sahih Muslim and Ibn Majah.

cxi Narrated by Abu Hurayrah, recorded by Fath Al-Bari.

cxii Narrated by Abu Al-'Aliyah, Ar-Rabi' and Qatadah, recorded by Ibn Abi Hatim.

cxiii Narrated by Al-Hasan Al-Basri.

cxiv Narrated by Al-Bara'.

cxv Narrated by Al-Bara' bin 'Azib, recorded by Sahih Al-Bukhari; also recorded by Sahih Muslim with a different chain of narrators.

cxvi Narrated by 'Aishah (the Prophet's wife), recorded by Imam Ahmad.

cxvii Narrated by Abu Sa'id, recorded by Imam Ahmad.

cxviii Narrated by Abul-Aswad, recorded by Imam Ahmad.

cxix Narrated by Abul-'Aliyah, recorded by Ibn Abi Hatim.

cxx Narrated by Anas, recorded by Imam Ahmad.

cxxi Recorded by Sahih Muslim.

cxxii Narrated by 'Abdur-Rahman bin Zayd bin Aslam, recorded by Ibn Abi Hatim.

cxxiii Recorded by Sahih Muslim.

cxxiv Narrated by Umm Salamah, recorded by Imam Ahmad.

cxxv Narrated by Umm Salamah, recorded by Imam Ahmad.

cxxvi Narrated by Ash-Sha'bi.

cxxvii Narrated by Jabir, recorded by Sahih Muslim.

cxxviii Narrated by Abu Al-'Aliyah, recorded by Ibn Abi Hatim.

cxxix Narrated by Abu Hurayrah, recorded by Imam Ahmad.

cxxx Narrated by Asma' bint Yazid bin As-Sakan, recorded by Abu Dawud.

cxxxi Narrated by 'Abdullah bin Mas'ud, recorded by Sahih Muslim and Fath Al-Bari.

cxxxii Recorded by Sahih Muslim.

cxxxiii Narrated by Qatadah and As-Suddi, recorded by Ibn Abi Hatim.

cxxxiv Narrated by Ibn 'Abbas.

cxxxv Recorded by Imam Ahmad, Al-Muwatta, Abu Dawud, Tuhfat Al-Ahwadhi, An-Nasai and Ibn Majah.

cxxxvi Recorded by al-Qurtubi.

cxxxvii Narrated by Ibn 'Umar, recorded by Imam Ahmad, Ibn Majah and Ad-Daraqutni.

cxxxviii Narrated by Masruq, recorded by As-Sunan Al-Kubra.

cxxxix Narrated by Abu Al-'Aliyah, recorded by Ibn Abi Hatim.

cxl Recorded by Imam Ahmad.

cxli Narrated by Abu Hurayrah, recorded by Sahih Muslim and Fath Al-Bari.

cxlii Narrated by 'Ali, recorded by Sahih Al-Bukhari.

cxliii The Four Imams – Abu Hanifah, Malik, Shafi'i and Ahmad.

cxliv Narrated by Ibn 'Umar, recorded by Sahih Muslim and Fath Al-Bari.

cxlv Narrated by Abu Hurayrah, recorded by 'Abdur-Razzaq.

cxlvi Narrated by Ibn 'Abbas, recorded by At-Tabari.

cxlvii Narrated by 'Aisha, recorded by Sahih Muslim and Fath Al-Bari.

[cxlviii] Narrated by Ibn 'Abbas, recorded by Fath Al-Bari.

[cxlix] Narrated by Wathilah bin Al-Asqa', recorded by Imam Ahmad.

[cl] Recorded by Sahih Muslim.

[cli] Narrated by Jabir, recorded by Sahih Muslim and Fath Al-Bari.

[clii] Narrated by Abu Sa'id, recorded by Imam Ahmad.

[cliii] Recorded by Sahih Muslim.

[cliv] Narrated by Abu Hurayrah, recorded by Imam Ahmad, Ibn Majah and Tuhfat Al-Ahwadhi.

[clv] Narrated by Abu Ishaq, recorded by Fath Al-Bari.

[clvi] Narrated by 'A'ishah, recorded by Sahih Muslim.

[clvii] Narrated by Anas, recorded by Sahih Muslim.

[clviii] Narrated by 'Amr bin Al-'As, recorded by Imam Ahmad.

[clix] Narrated by Abu Sa'id, recorded by Imam Ahmad.

[clx] Narrated by Abu Hurayrah, recorded by Imam Ahmad.

[clxi] Narrated by Ibn 'Abbas, recorded by At-Tabari.

[clxii] Narrated by Ibn 'Abbas, recorded by At-Tabari.

[clxiii] Narrated by Qatadah, recorded by At-Tabari.

[clxiv] Narrated by Ibn 'Umar, recorded by 'Abdur-Razzaq; this hadith was also recorded by Al-Hakim in his Mustadrak.

[clxv] Narrated by Al-Hasan, recorded by Ibn Abi Hatim.

[clxvi] Narrated by Abu Al-'Aliyah, recorded by At-Tabari.

[clxvii] Narrated by Buraydah, recorded by Sahih Muslim.

[clxviii] Narrated by Ibn 'Umar, recorded by Sahih Muslim and Fath Al-Bari; there are many more hadiths on this subject.

[clxix] Recorded by Sahih Muslim and Fath Al-Bari.

[clxx] Narrated by Jabir bin 'Abdullah, recorded by Imam Ahmad.

[clxxi] Narrated by 'Abdur-Razzaq,

[clxxii] Narrated by Ibn 'Abbas, recorded by Ibn Abi Hatim.

[clxxiii] Narrated by Al-Hujjaj bin 'Amr Al-Ansari, recorded by Imam Ahmad.

[clxxiv] Narrated by Ka'b, recorded by Fath Al-Bari.

[clxxv] Narrated by Ibn 'Umar, recorded by At-Tabari.

[clxxvi] Narrated by Ibn 'Umar, recorded by At-Tabari.

[clxxvii] Narrated by Ibn 'Abbas, recorded by At-Tabari.

[clxxviii] Narrated by Ibn 'Abbas, recorded by Al-Umm; another hadith states: "No Ihram for Hajj should be assumed, except during the months of Hajj" [Narrated by Ibn 'Abbas, recorded by Ibn Khuzaymah].

[clxxix] There are several hadiths on this: narrated by 'Abdullah bin 'Umar, 'Ata' bin Abu Rabah, 'Amr bin Dinar (and many more), recorded by At-Tabari.

[clxxx] Narrated by Abu Hurayrah, recorded by Sahih Muslim and Fath Al-Bari.

[clxxxi] Narrated by 'Abdur-Rahman bin Ya'mar Ad-Diyli, recorded by Imam Ahmad, Abu Dawud, Tuhfat Al-Ahwadhi, An-Nasa'i and Ibn Majah.

[clxxxii] Narrated by Ibn 'Umar, recorded by Ibn Abi Hatim.

[clxxxiii] Narrated by Ibn 'Umar, recorded by At-Tabari.

[clxxxiv] Al-Hums means 'strictly religious' as the Quraysh were called because they used to say that they were the people of Allah and they did not go out of the sanctuary.

[clxxxv] Narrated by A'ishah, recorded by Fath Al-Bari; this has also been narrated by Ibn 'Abbas, Mujahid, 'Ata', Qatadah and As-Suddi, recorded by At-Tabari.

[clxxxvi] Recorded by Sahih Muslim and Fath Al-Bari.

[clxxxvii] Narrated by Shaddad bin Aws, recorded by Fath Al-Bari.

[clxxxviii] Narrated by Ibn 'Abbas, recorded by Ibn Abi Hatim.

[clxxxix] Narrated by Ibn 'Abbas, recorded by Al-Qurtubi.

[cxc] Narrated by 'Uqbah bin 'Amr, recorded by Imam Ahmad.

[cxci] Narrated by 'Ikrimah, recorded by Ibn Abi Hatim.

[cxcii] Narrated by 'Abdullah bin Hudhafah, recorded by At-Tabari.

[cxciii] Recorded by Fath Al-Bari.

[cxciv] Narrated by 'Aishah, recorded by Fath Al-Bari.

[cxcv] Narrated by Ibn Jarir, recorded by At-Tabari.

[cxcvi] Recorded by Fath Al-Bari.

[cxcvii] Narrated by Ibn Jarir, recorded by At-Tabari.

[cxcviii] Narrated by Qatadah, recorded by 'Abdur-Razzaq.

[cxcix] Narrated by Ibn Wahb, recorded by At-Tabari.

[cc] Narrated by Abu Hurayrah, recorded by 'Abdur-Razzaq.

[cci] Narrated by Khabbab bin Al-Aratt, recorded by Fath Al-Bari.

[ccii] Narrated by Muqatil bin Hayyan, recorded by Ibn Abi Hatim.

[cciii] Recorded by Al-Hakim.

[cciv] Reported by Az-Zuhri.

[ccv] Recorded by Sahih Muslim.

[ccvi] Narrated by Abu Maysarah, recorded by Imam Ahmad.

[ccvii] Narrated by Jabir, recorded by Sahih Muslim.

[ccviii] Narrated by Ibn 'Abbas, recorded by At-Tabari.

[ccix] Recorded by Fath Al-Bari.

[ccx] Narrated by Ibn 'Amr, recorded by Sahih Muslim.

[ccxi] Narrated by Abu Hurayrah, recorded by Sahih Muslim and Fath Al-Bari.

[ccxii] Recorded by Sahih Muslim.

[ccxiii] Narrated by Maymunah bint Al-Harith Al-Hilaliyah, recorded by Sahih Muslim and Fath Al-Bari.

[ccxiv] Narrated by Ibn 'Abbas, recorded by At-Tabari.

[ccxv] Narrated by Ibn 'Abbas, recorded by Fath Al-Bari.

[ccxvi] Narrated by Ibn 'Abbas, recorded by Tuhfat Al-Ahwadhi, An-Nasa'i and Sahih Ibn Hibban.

[ccxvii] Narrated by Ibn 'Abbas, recorded by At-Tabari (there are several other chains that support this hadith).

[ccxviii] Narrated by Abu Hurayrah, recorded by Sahih Muslim.

[ccxix] Narrated by Ibn 'Abbas, recorded by Ibn Abi Hatim.

[ccxx] Narrated by Ibn 'Abbas, recorded by Ibn Abi Hatim.

[ccxxi] Narrated by 'Abdullah bin 'Umar, recorded by Al-Muwatta.

[ccxxii] Narrated by 'Umar, recorded by At-Tabari.

[ccxxiii] Narrated by Jabir, recorded by Sahih Muslim.

[ccxxiv] Narrated by Mu'awiyah bin Haydah Al-Qushayri, recorded by Abu Dawud.

[ccxxv] Narrated by Ibn 'Abbas, recorded by At-Tabari.

[ccxxvi] Narrated by Mahmud bin Labid, recorded by An-Nasa'i.

[ccxxvii] Hadith recorded by Al-Muwatta.

[ccxxviii] Narrated by Ibn Jarir, recorded by At-Tabari.

[ccxxix] Narrated by 'Abdullah bin Mas'ud, recorded by Imam Ahmad.

[ccxxx] Narrated by Ibn 'Abbas, Mujahid, Masruq, Al-Hassan, Qatadah, Ad-Dahhak, Ar-Rabi', and Muqatil bin Hayyan, recorded by Ibn Abi Hatim.

[ccxxxi] Recorded by Abu Dawud, At-Tirmidhi, Ibn Abu Hatim, Ibn Jarir and Ibn Marduwyah and Al-Bayhaqi.

[ccxxxii] Narrated by Ibn Marduwyah, recorded by Al-Bayhaqi.

[ccxxxiii] Narrated by Ad-Dahhak, recorded by At-Tabari.

[ccxxxiv] Narrated by Ibn Mas'ud, recorded by Sahih Muslim and Fath Al-Bari.

[ccxxxv] Narrated by 'Amr bin Al-'As, recorded by Imam Ahmad, Abu Dawud and Ibn Majah.

[ccxxxvi] Narrated by Umm Habibah and Zaynab bint Jahsh, recorded by Sahih Muslim and Fath Al-Bari.

[ccxxxvii] Narrated by Ibn 'Abbas, recorded by At-Tabari.

[ccxxxviii] Narrated by Ibn 'Abbas, recorded by At-Tabari.

[ccxxxix] Narrated by 'Ubaydah, recorded by Ibn Abi Hatim.

[ccxl] Narrated by Ibn 'Abbas, recorded by At-Tabari.

[ccxli] Narrated by Ibn Mas'ud, recorded by Sahih Muslim and Fath Al-Bari.

[ccxlii] Narrated by Ibn 'Umar, recorded by Sahih Muslim.

[ccxliii] Narrated by Buraydah bin Al-Husayb, recorded by Ibn Majah.

[ccxliv] Narrated by Mu'awiyah bin Hakam As-Sulami, recorded by Sahih Muslim.

[ccxlv] Narrated by Nafi', recorded by Sahih Muslim and Fath Al-Bari.

[ccxlvi] In Al-Bukhari in a chapter entitled: Prayer while confronting the forts and facing the enemy.

[ccxlvii] Narrated by 'Abdur-Rahman bin 'Awf, recorded by Imam Ahmad.

[ccxlviii] Recorded by Tahdhib At-Tahdhib.

[ccxlix] It has been stated in Ibn Kathir's Stories of the Prophets that the Philistines captured the ark and brought it to their city and they placed it beside their idol called Dagon.

[ccl] Narrated by Ibn Jurayj, recorded by At-Tabari. It has also been stated by As-Suddi that, 'The Tabut was brought to Talut's house, so the people believed in the Prophethood of Sham'un (Simeon) and obeyed Talut'.

[ccli] Narrated by As-Suddi, recorded by At-Tabari.

[cclii] Narrated by Ibn 'Abbas, recorded by At-Tabari.

[ccliii] Narrated by Ibn Jarir, stated in Ibn Kathir's Stories of the Prophets, page 484.

[ccliv] Ibn Kathir's Stories of the Prophets, page 483.

[cclv] Narrated by Abu Dharr, recorded by Sahih Ibn Hibban.

[cclvi] Narrated by Abu Hurayrah, recorded by Sahih Muslim and Fath Al-Bari.

[cclvii] Narrated by 'Ubayy bin Ka'b, recorded by Imam Ahmad.

[cclviii] Recorded by Abu Dawud, Ibn Majah and Tuhfat Al-Ahwadhi.

[cclix] Narrated by Abu Musa, recorded by Sahih Muslim.

[cclx] Recorded by Sahih Muslim.

[cclxi] Narrated by Ibn 'Abbas, recorded by At-Tabari.

[cclxii] Narrated by Ibn 'Abbas, recorded by Ibn Abi Hatim.

[cclxiii] Narrated by Ibn 'Abbas, recorded by At-Tabari.

[cclxiv] Narrated by Mujahid, recorded by At-Tabari.

[cclxv] Narrated by As-Suddi, recorded by At-Tabari.

[cclxvi] Stories of the Prophets, page 150.

[cclxvii] Narrated by Qatadah, Suddi and Ibn Ishaq, from the Stories of the Prophets, page 151.

[cclxviii] Narrated by Zaid bin Aslam, Stories of the Prophets, page 152 to 153.

[cclxix] Narrated by As-Suddi, recorded by At-Tabari.

[cclxx] Narrated by Ibn 'Abbas, recorded by Al-Qurtubi.

[cclxxi] Narrated by Abu Mas'ud, recorded by Imam Ahmad.

[cclxxii] Narrated by Abu Hurayrah, recorded by Imam Ahmad.

[cclxxiii] Narrated by Abu Dharr, recorded by Sahih Muslim.

[cclxxiv] Recorded by Al-Hakim.

[cclxxv] Narrated by Ibn 'Abbas, recorded by At-Tabari.

[cclxxvi] Narrated by Ibn Mas'ud, recorded by Imam Ahmad.

[cclxxvii] Recorded by Abu Dawud.

[cclxxviii] Narrated by Abu Hurayrah, recorded by Sahih Muslim and Fath Al-Bari.

[cclxxix] Narrated by 'Ata' Al-Khurasani, recorded by Ibn Abi Hatim.

[cclxxx] Narrated by Abu Hurayrah, recorded by Sahih Muslim and Fath Al-Bari.

[cclxxxi] Narrated by Abu Hurayrah, recorded by Fath Al-Bari.

[cclxxxii] Narrated by Abu Sa'id, recorded by Imam Ahmad.

[cclxxxiii] Narrated by Sa'd bin Abi Waqqas, recorded by Sahih Muslim and Fath Al-Bari.

[cclxxxiv] Narrated by Abu Mas'ud, recorded by Imam Ahmad.

[cclxxxv] Narrated by 'Ali and Ibn Mas'ud, recorded by Sahih Muslim.

[cclxxxvi] Narrated by Samurah bin Jundub, recorded by Fath Al-Bari.

[cclxxxvii] Recorded by Abu Dawud.

[cclxxxviii] Narrated by 'Umar, recorded by Imam Ahmad and Ibn Majah.

[cclxxxix] Narrated by An-Nu'man bin Bashir, recorded by Sahih Muslim and Fath Al-Bari.

[ccxc] Narrated by 'Abdullah bin Mas'ud, recorded by At-Tabari; this was similarly reported by Imam Ahmad.

[ccxci] Narrated by Abu Hurayrah, recorded by Fath Al-Bari.

ccxcii Narrated by Ibn 'Abbas, recorded by At-Tabari.

ccxciii Narrated by 'Amr bin Al-Ahwas, recorded by Ibn Abi Hatim.

ccxciv Narrated by Sulayman bin Buraydah, recorded by Imam Ahmad.

ccxcv Narrated by Hudhayfah, recorded by Fath Al-Bari, Sahih Muslim and Ibn Majah.

ccxcvi Narrated by Abu Hurayrah, recorded by Sahih Muslim.

ccxcvii Narrated by Ash-Sha'bi, recorded by Ibn Abi Hatim.

ccxcviii Narrated by Qatadah, recorded by Imam Ahmad, Abu Dawud, Tuhfat Al-Ahwadhi, An-Nasa'i and Ibn Majah.

ccxcix Narrated by Ibn 'Abbas.

ccc Narrated by Ibn 'Abbas, recorded by Imam Ahmad.

ccci Narrated by Abu Hurayrah, recorded by Fath Al-Bari, Sahih Muslim, Abu Dawud, Tuhfat Al-Ahwadhi, An-Nasa'i and Ibn Majah.

cccii Narrated by Abu Hurayrah, recorded by Sahih Muslim and Fath Al-Bari.

ccciii Narrated by 'Abdullah, recorded by Sahih Muslim.

ccciv Narrated by Ibn 'Abbas, recorded by Sahih Muslim and An-Nasa'i.

cccv Narrated by Abu Mas'ud, recorded by Fath Al-Bari.

cccvi Narrated by Ibn Jarir, recorded by At-Tabari.

Made in the USA
Columbia, SC
11 May 2024

35577826R00117